ECONOMIC PERSPECTIVES ON AFFIRMATIVE ACTION

Economic Perspectives on Affirmative Action

M.V. Lee Badgett

Andrew F. Brimmer

Cecilia A. Conrad

Heidi I. Hartmann

Edited by Margaret C. Simms

Joint Center for Political and Economic Studies
Washington, D.C.

The Joint Center gratefully acknowledges the support of the Ford and Rockefeller foundations in helping to make this publication possible.

Distributed by arrangement with
University Press of America
4720 Boston Way
Lanham, MD 20706

Library of Congress Cataloging-in-Publication Data:

Economic perspectives on affirmative action / Andrew F. Brimmer, Cecilia A. Conrad, M.V. Lee Badgett, Heidi I. Hartmann; edited by Margaret C. Simms.
        p.   cm.
Includes bibliographical references.
ISBN 0-8191-9932-X (alk. paper).— ISBN 0-8191-9931-1 (pbk.: alk. paper)
1. Affirmative action programs—United States—Compliance costs.
2. Afro-Americans—Employment—Government policy—Compliance costs.
3. Discrimination in employment—Economic aspects—United States.
I. Brimmer, Andrew F.   II. Simms, Margaret C.
HF5549.5.A34E28 1995
331.13'3'0973—dc20

                                                    95-9008
                                                    CIP

FOREWORD

Most Americans would like to have a society that provides equal opportunity for all its citizens, but there is no consensus on the policies or means of achieving that goal. The current public debate on affirmative action illustrates the diversity of opinion surrounding this issue. Unfortunately, the politically charged environment in which the debate is being carried out has served more to confuse than to enlighten the public concerning the goals, strategies, and objectives of the nation's affirmative action policies and practices.

Some opponents of affirmative action have cast all its strategies in terms of reverse discrimination, asserting that they give preferential treatment to members of targeted groups—women, blacks, and other racial-ethnic minorities—including persons who might not otherwise be qualified for the opportunities they obtain under these programs. At the other end of the spectrum are supporters of affirmative action who refuse to consider any need for review or any change in the number or structure of its programs. Of course, the reality is often more complicated than the image presented by either side. Our hope is that by providing information to clarify the issues, we can help the nation move toward a more rational discussion of the subject.

Today's debate is not unique in many respects. During the past fifteen years, the policies related to affirmative action have been called into question at least three times: first, in the early 1980s, when Ronald Reagan assumed the presidency and initiated changes in executive branch oversight of companies' employment practices; again in the late 1980s, when several key Supreme Court decisions, among them *Ward's Cove* v. *Atonio* and *Patterson* v. *McLean Credit Union,* narrowed affirmative action's scope (but before passage of the Civil Rights Restoration Act); and finally in 1995, when federal and state policymakers began to call for its review or repeal. In each instance, the Joint Center for Political and Economic Studies has contributed to the public dialogue by providing information and statistical analysis on the program structure and effectiveness of various affirmative action initiatives.

With the support of the Ford Foundation, the Joint Center began a long-term study of group-sensitive remedies in both the employment and minority business areas. Several publications have been issued since that effort began, but none has turned out to be more timely than this one. I would like to thank the Ford Foundation for its support of the group-sensitive remedies project and both the Ford and Rockefeller foundations for their overall support of the Joint Center. The work has been conducted under the supervision of Dr. Milton D. Morris, vice president for research, and Dr. Margaret C. Simms, director of research programs. To them, as well as the contributing authors of this important new volume, we are very grateful.

Eddie N. Williams
President
Joint Center for Political
and Economic Studies

CONTENTS

LIST OF TABLES

About the Authors

M.V. Lee Badgett is a labor economist and assistant professor of public affairs at the University of Maryland, College Park. Her current research is concerned with the labor market effects of race, gender, and sexual orientation, including a focus on antidiscrimination policy and affirmative action.

Andrew F. Brimmer is president of Brimmer & Company, Inc., a Washington D.C.-based economic and financial consulting firm, and the Wilmer D. Barrett Professor of Economics at the University of Massachusetts, Amherst. Dr. Brimmer formerly served as a member of the Board of Governors of the Federal Reserve System. His analysis of the economic burden that racial discrimination places on interstate commerce was cited as evidence by the U.S. Supreme Court in its decision to uphold the Public Accommodations sections of the Civil Rights Act of 1964.

Cecilia A. Conrad is associate professor of economics at Barnard College, Columbia University. Her teaching and research focus on the ways public policy influences the economic status of minorities and women. Dr. Conrad's published articles have addressed a variety of topics, including school choice, the feminization of poverty, and the measurement of racial inequalities in income.

Heidi I. Hartmann is the cofounder and director of the Washington-based Institute for Women's Policy Research, and was formerly director of Women's Studies at Rutgers University. An economist whose work has covered a wide range of issues, her research at the National Academy of Sciences on pay equity helped establish comparable worth as a remedy for the underpayment of women. In 1994, Dr. Hartmann was the recipient of a MacArthur Fellowship.

Margaret C. Simms is director of research programs at the Joint Center for Political and Economic Studies. Her work as an economist has included research and evaluation of education, employment and training, and minority business development programs. For five years, Dr. Simms served as editor of *The Review of Black Political Economy.*

INTRODUCTION

Margaret C. Simms

INTRODUCTION

I n the 30 years since passage of the Civil Rights Act of 1964, there has been considerable change in American society. However, one of the policies flowing from that Act—affirmative action—remains a source of some controversy among policy analysts, litigators, and the general public. The policy was molded and modified over four presidential administrations, from Lyndon Johnson's to Jimmy Carter's. Two of its more controversial features, goals and timetables, were instituted under a Republican President, Richard Nixon.

Affirmative action came under direct attack during the first two years of the Reagan administration, but opponents of the policy within that administration soon discovered that its impact could be more quickly limited through benign neglect. During the 1980s, enforcement levels tended to decline, in part because the resources of both the Office of Federal Contract Compliance and the Equal Employment Opportunity Commission were reduced. Moreover, strategies were changed. Individual complaints were pursued rather than the class-action cases that have an impact on more people.

In 1989, the U.S. Supreme Court handed down a series of rulings whose general effect was to narrow the range of evidence allowable in proving discrimination, making the justification of affirmative action programs more difficult and calling into question the construction of broad remedies such as affirmative action. Over the next two years Congress tried to pass legislation to restore equal employment practice and litigation to the standards that had evolved between 1964 and 1989. During the same period, conservative policymakers and advocates worked to defeat the pending Civil Rights Restoration Act. The conservatives lost that effort in 1991, and civil rights enforcement law in the area of employment was returned to a form that had become familiar to both the civil rights and business communities.

It should not be surprising that after the Civil Rights Restoration Act of 1991 was passed, public debate over affirmative action shifted from the legal issues to questions of cost and reverse discrimination. Conservatives alleged that this policy was contributing to the decline in U.S. economic power, both by lowering the average productivity of workers through the hiring of underqualified minorities and by increasing the cost of doing business with the regulatory burden of compliance. Moreover, some of them argued, affirmative action policies had not even helped the black community, since poverty and low incomes were as prevalent as—if not more prevalent than—they were 30 years ago.

Though fair criticism of affirmative action may be warranted and review of the effectiveness of specific programs is appropriate, these specific charges rest on weak foundations. To begin with, they assume an incorrect definition of the policy as it is mandated and generally practiced. Affirmative action is a term that has been applied to many public and private initiatives designed to address problems of discrimination or exclusion in employment.[1] At one end of the spectrum, the term is used in conjunction with pursuit of equal employment or anti-discrimination laws—that is, merely ensuring that candidates for employment are treated fairly. It is perhaps more appropriately applied to strategies in which firms "act affirmatively" to include members of protected classes in the pool of candidates for positions through expansion of recruitment networks, review of qualifications to determine that they are necessary to perform the job, and so on.

Opponents of affirmative action sometimes state or imply that affirmative action means the setting of rigid quotas and the placement of unqualified people in positions merely because they meet these quotas, or that it means the overt preference of any member of a protected class over any member who is not in a protected class. However, neither laws nor government regulations apply any of these requirements to corporations or other institutions. The one exception is when a court order for remedial action is issued as the result of a legal finding of past discrimination. In some cases, quotas are set by the courts, and companies are expected to establish hiring procedures that enable them to reach those quotas, though they are not required to hire unqualified people in order to do so. Companies sometimes voluntarily set employment goals based on the availability of different groups in the labor pool from which they draw workers, but there are no sanctions if a company fails to meet its goals.

The studies/essays presented in this volume offer three perspectives on the issue of affirmative action, and collectively they challenge many of the assumptions and criticisms raised about its impact.

In "The Economic Cost of Discrimination Against Black Americans," Andrew Brimmer calculates the loss to our economy, in dollars, resulting from blacks' not being employed to their full capacity and not receiving education and training commensurate with that received by their white counterparts. Brimmer estimates that in 1993 the disparate treatment of blacks cost the U.S. economy $241 billion—3.8 percent of gross domestic product—a cost that has grown over time. More than one-half of this continuing GDP loss is due to the failure to employ blacks in jobs that use their *current* skills, suggesting that instead of being in jobs that exceed their qualifications many blacks are *over*-qualified for the jobs they actually hold. While Brimmer's analysis focuses only on the black labor force, similar analyses could be completed on many other groups covered by equal employment laws. The GDP cost to society of not using individuals to their full potential—or equivalent measures of it— is usually missing in today's public discussions of affirmative action, an irony given critics' charge that the policy itself has been too costly to implement.

In "The Economic Cost of Affirmative Action," Cecilia Conrad takes on the conservatives' economic-efficiency arguments directly. She esti- mates the policy's direct costs, both in public expenditure (enforcement) and private expenditure (compliance), and examines as well the impact affirmative-action hiring has on productivity in a number of industries. Conrad's analysis leads her to the conclusion that direct costs of enforcing affirmative action are quite small relative to the cost of doing business, on the order of $12 per employee per year, and also finds that the impact on productivity appears to be minimal.

In "The Effectiveness of Equal Employment Opportunity Policies," M. V. Lee Badgett and Heidi Hartmann review studies of the effectiveness of affirmative action. These studies use different approaches and method- ologies. In some cases the researchers measure equal employment/ affirmative action activity by comparing firms that are subject to high standards of federal review (such as contractors) with those that are not.

In other cases, the wages, employment, and/or occupational status of minority groups and women are reviewed for comparison between the period before equal employment laws took effect and afterwards. In spite of these differences in approach and frequent limitations in the data available, there is a consistency in the findings regarding the impact on wages, employment, and occupational status. In sum, Badgett and Hartmann conclude, the preponderance of evidence suggests that activity associated with equal employment and affirmative action policies is associated with small but significant gains in wages and employment by people of color and women in a range of blue-collar and white-collar occupations.[2] Moreover, they find no evidence that these gains were made at the expense of either firm competitiveness or fair employment practices. It appears that many of the jobs gained by minorities and women were the result of garnering a greater share of new jobs created and not the result of displacing white males.

While all three studies included in this volume support the position that affirmative action has had some positive effects on the employment position of protected classes and limited negative effects on other workers and firm productivity, they find the measurable benefits to individuals to be quite small. For example, Badgett and Hartmann point to the continued differential in unemployment rates between blacks and whites, and Brimmer notes the persistence of occupational disparities. The authors point out that affirmative action can reduce some forms of discrimination, but does not necessarily eliminate institutional or systemic discrimination.

The review of the evidence would lead one to conclude that while affirmative action can be an effective policy tool, its impact is related to the vigor with which it is enforced. Moreover, it does not hold the power to overcome other economic forces, nor can this one tool eliminate all racial or gender disparities. In sum, it can only be one strategy within a larger policy agenda to promote equity in American society.

1. The term is sometimes applied to other race/gender remedies such as minority business programs, but has historically been used for employment programs flowing out of Executive Order No. 11246, which required that government contractors "take affirmative action to ensure that employees are treated during employment without regard to their race, creed, color, or national origin." (See the Proclamation of President Lyndon Johnson in "Executive Order 11246," *Federal Register,* Vol. 30, 24 September 1965, p. 12319.)

2. The gains are "significant" in the statistical meaning of the term, that is, they are attributable to the equal employment/affirmative action policies.

THE ECONOMIC COST OF DISCRIMINATION AGAINST BLACK AMERICANS

Andrew F. Brimmer

THE ECONOMIC COST OF DISCRIMINATION AGAINST BLACK AMERICANS

T he disparate treatment of blacks cost the American economy about $241 billion in 1993. This figure is equal to roughly 3.8 percent of that year's gross domestic product (GDP). While part of the loss can be attributed to the lag in blacks' educational achievement, the bulk of the shortfall appears to be related to continued discrimination, which limits their access to higher-paying jobs. Furthermore, over the last quarter-century, the relative cost of discrimination seems to have risen. And, given the slow rate at which blacks are being absorbed into managerial, professional, and technical positions, the income deficit they face—and the corresponding economic cost to the nation—will probably narrow very little in the years ahead.

ECONOMIC IMPACT OF RACIAL DISCRIMINATION

The earliest assessment of the economic cost of discrimination against nonwhites in the United States was prepared by the President's Council of Economic Advisers (CEA) in 1962.1 The CEA estimated the cost at approximately $17.8 billion, or 3.2 percent of gross national product (GNP)—which totaled $554.9 billion in that year. (Note that GNP, the value of total production of goods and services measured at market prices, was the official measure of economic activity in use in 1962.)

In 1965, when I was assistant secretary of commerce, at my request the U.S. Bureau of the Census made estimates of the cost of discrimination

Note: An earlier version of this paper was presented before the North American Economics and Finance Association and the National Economic Association on January 5, 1993.

against nonwhites for the years 1949 through 1963. The Census Bureau's estimating procedure was more comprehensive than that employed earlier by the CEA. The Cenus Bureau's estimates sought to account for the economic losses originating from two sources: inefficiencies in the use of the labor force arising from failure to use fully the *existing* education, skills, and experience of the population, and failure to develop fully *potential* education, skills, and experience. The losses were described in terms of the gains that might accrue to GNP if discrimination were eliminated—or had been eliminated in the past. However, the Census Bureau recognized that, because the legacy of past discrimination affects the contemporary occupational, geographic, and capital structures as well as the education, training, and skills of the nonwhite labor force, the gains would accrue only over time as the labor force is upgraded and the economy adjusts.

Based on the Census Bureau's analysis described above, I estimated that discrimination against nonwhites cost about $20.1 billion in lost GNP in 1963, equal to 3.5 percent of that year's total GNP of $583.9 billion. Roughly $11.1 billion (1.9 percent of GNP) reflected the failure to use fully nonwhites' existing skills, and $9.0 billion (1.6 percent of GNP) arose from the failure to improve and fully use their educational achievement.[2]

Applying the Census Bureau's technique as used in 1965, I have recently updated the estimates for the economic cost of discrimination against blacks. The detailed results for four years (1967, 1973, 1979, and 1993) are shown in Appendix Tables A.1 and A.2.

TRENDS IN THE ECONOMIC COST OF DISCRIMINATION

The figures show that, over the last 25 years or so, the American economy has been losing between 1.5 percent and 2.2 percent of GDP because racial discrimination against blacks limits the full use of their existing educational attainment. In 1967, this loss amounted to 1.5 percent of GDP or $12.1 billion (Table 1). Another 1.4 percent ($11.1 billion) of GDP was lost because of the failure to *improve* and fully utilize blacks' educational level. In combination, lost GDP amounted to $23.2 billion, equal to 2.9 percent of the 1967 total of $814.3 billion. By 1993, the shortfall in GDP due to the failure to use blacks' existing education amounted to $137.5 billion (2.2 percent of GDP). Failure to improve their education cost $103.9 billion (1.6 percent). The aggregate loss was estimated at $240.9 billion—3.8 percent of GDP.

The statistics in Table 1 enable one to apportion the loss in GDP between contemporary discrimination against blacks (failure to use fully their existing education) and the legacy of past discrimination (failure to improve their education). The figures suggest that, while no dramatic shifts have occurred over the last two and a half decades, the proportion of the loss that can be attributed to current discrimination has risen slightly. The latter component varied from 52.2 percent in 1967, to 54.31 percent in 1973, to 54.44 percent in 1979, and to 56.87 percent in 1993.

FACTORS CONTRIBUTING TO THE COST OF RACIAL DISCRIMINATION

A number of interwoven factors lie behind the loss of GDP from racial discrimination. In the first instance, discrimination has historically restricted many blacks to working in positions in which they could not fully utilize their qualifications. For example, for many years, the U.S. Postal Service employed thousands of black men with college degrees in mathematics, chemistry, and other sciences who could not find jobs in the private sector. There were numerous cases where blacks with B.A. and M.A. degrees in business administration worked as warehouse and stockroom clerks—while their white counterparts held managerial jobs in areas such as banking, insurance, and real estate. Even today, despite the lessening of restrictions because of equal opportunity laws and the spread of affirmative action practices in industry, many blacks are still concentrated in positions which do not make full use of their talents. If racial discrimination were to be eliminated, blacks could migrate more freely from low to high productivity occupations where their contribution to total production would be increased. The result would be a gain in the nation's total output of goods and services.

Furthermore, a more rational use of the labor force most likely would require increased investment in the stock of capital. Plant and equipment outlays would rise—further boosting the gain in output. Thus, capital as well as labor incomes would be enhanced.

Self-employed entrepreneurs (particularly blacks) would have greater access to markets—and thus, become more efficient—in the absence of racial discrimination. In response, their incomes would rise to reflect their higher productivity. This is another source of the gain in GDP resulting from the elimination of racial discrimination.

LONG-TERM OUTLOOK

There appears to be little likelihood that the economic cost of racial discrimination will diminish appreciably over the current decade. While overt acts of discrimination in industry will almost certainly continue to decline, institutional or systemic discrimination will nevertheless persist due to the legacy of previous discrimination. Consequently, blacks' educational levels will remain well below those of whites, and they will continue to be underrepresented in the higher-paying positions and overrepresented in those at the low end of the occupational scale. The net result will be a continuation of large deficits in blacks' employment and income. The latter will continue to be translated directly into a sizeable loss in GDP.

The significant gap between blacks' educational attainment and that of the nation at large can be seen in Table 2. The figures compare the distribution of black workers by years of school completed with the corresponding distribution of all workers in 1990. It will be noted that, while blacks represented 10.15 percent of total employment, they accounted for 13.29 percent of workers with less than a high school education. At the high school level, they represented 11.13 percent of the total. The black proportion was 10.53 percent among workers with one to three years of college, and 6.22 percent among those with four or more years of college. Expressed differently, in 1990, 45.5 percent of all workers had at least some college education compared with 37.0 percent of all black workers. The weighted average number of years of schooling for all workers combined was 13.29. The corresponding weighted average for blacks was 12.66 years. This meant that the typical black worker's average level of education lagged about 4.75 percent behind that of all workers. Although the differential will probably narrow somewhat, it most likely will not be closed any time soon.

In a similar vein, blacks will continue to hold a disproportionately small share of the high-ranking occupations. The occupational profiles of blacks and all employees in 1990 are shown in Tables 3A and 3B. A projection by the U.S. Bureau of Labor Statistics (BLS) for all workers for the year 2005 is also shown—along with Brimmer & Company's estimate for blacks in the same year.

Several features stand out: While blacks represented 10.0 percent of total occupational employment in 1990, they fell progressively short of that proportion as one moved up the occupational scale. At the opposite end of the spectrum, their actual shares were 1.5 to 1.7 times their proportion of total employment. By the year 2005, BLS projections suggest that blacks' overall occupational profile will probably have changed only moderately. They will then hold about 11.1 percent of all jobs. Using this benchmark, blacks will have raised their already above-par share of administrative and clerical positions, and they will be near parity with respect to technical and related jobs. They will also have narrowed slightly the gaps between parity and their actual holdings of managerial and professional occupations. Nevertheless, blacks will still be overrepresented in jobs at the foot of the occupational ladder.

The foregoing black employment and occupational disparities translate into large and persistent deficits in blacks' share of money income. The scope of these disparities is shown in Table 4. The statistics describe estimates and projections of the U.S. population, civilian labor force, employment, and money income, by race, for the years 1991, 1992, 1993, and 2000. It will be noted that, in each year, blacks' labor force share, employment share, and income share all fall short of their share of the total population. Moreover, in each case, the size of the gap is projected to narrow only slightly over the remainder of this decade.

The magnitude of the disparity in blacks' money income can be seen in Table 5. For example, it is estimated that in 1993 blacks received $300.7 billion in money income, equal to 7.6 percent of total money income received. This amount represented a sizeable deficit in the income of the black community—no matter what benchmark is used to measure parity. If blacks' share of population is used as the yardstick, the shortfall was $192.3 billion, or 39.1 percent. Using their share of the civilian labor force, the income gap was $134.5 billion, or 30.9 percent; by share of employment, it was $103.7 billion, or 25.6 percent.

It is estimated that, in the year 2000, blacks' income may amount to $455.2 billion. This figure would represent 7.95 percent of the total. Again, if blacks' share of population is taken as parity, the income deficit would amount to $285.1 billion, equal to 38.52 percent. Using blacks' civilian labor force share as parity, the deficit would be $186.1 billion (29.02 percent), while using their employment share would produce a deficit of $135.6 billion, equal to 22.97 percent.

It should also be noted that all of the projected deficits in the year 2000 would be essentially unchanged in percentage terms compared with what they were in 1993.

The black income deficits also represent losses in GDP over and above those discussed earlier, because the income loss reduces consumption. As shown in Table 5, using blacks' population share as the parity benchmark, the income deficit was equal to 3.02 percent of GDP in 1993. With the labor force share as benchmark, it was 2.11 percent; and for employment, it was 1.63 percent. By the year 2000, these three parity measures are projected to yield income deficits equal to 3.19 percent, 2.08 percent, and 1.52 percent of GDP, respectively.

Again, it will be noted that black income deficits in relation to GDP remain essentially unchanged over the remainder of this decade. Thus, the economic cost of racial discrimination will continue as a major burden on the American economy.

CONCLUDING OBSERVATIONS

The analysis presented here has shown that, while blacks' educational attainment continues to fall short of that for the population as a whole, many blacks also continue to be employed in jobs well below what their actual education and skills would justify. To a considerable extent, these disparities mirror the effects of past—and present—racial discrimination.

The failure to use fully blacks' existing educational attainments—compounded by the failure to improve their educational levels—results in a sizeable shortfall in the money incomes earned by blacks. The income deficits can be translated into losses in GDP. Since the mid-1960s, these losses have represented between 3 percent and 4 percent of GDP. Thus, they provide a rough indication of the cost to the nation of discrimination against blacks.

Looking ahead, there is little reason to expect this cost to be diminished very much by the unaided operation of the labor market. Consequently, there is a continuing need for investment to improve blacks' education and skills. There is also a continuing need for vigorous affirmative action programs to eradicate the lingering racial discrimination in American industry.

NOTES

1. See Council of Economic Advisers, Press Release issued September 25, 1962.

2 See Andrew F. Brimmer, "The Negro in the American Economy."

TABLE 1

ECONOMIC COST OF DISCRIMINATION AGAINST BLACKS, 1967–93

(ESTIMATED LOSS OF GROSS DOMESTIC PRODUCT)

Amounts in Billions of Dollars

YEAR	GROSS DOMESTIC PRODUCT	GAIN FROM FULL USE OF PRESENT EDUCATION		GAIN FROM FULL USE OF IMPROVED EDUCATION		TOTAL GAIN FROM FULL USE OF PRESENT AND IMPROVED EDUCATION	
		amount	percent	amount	percent	amount	percent
1967	$ 814.30	$ 12.10	1.49%	$ 11.10	1.36%	$ 23.20	2.85%
1973	1,349.80	22.90	1.70	19.40	1.43	42.30	3.13
1979	2,488.60	45.80	1.84	38.20	1.53	84.00	3.38
1993	6,374.00	137.00	2.15	103.90	1.63	240.90	3.79

Source: Prepared by Brimmer & Company, Inc. Data for GDP from the U.S. Department of Commerce, Bureau of Economic Analysis. Percentage increases in compensation and other income estimated by Brimmer & Company, Inc., based on data from the U.S. Department of Commerce, Bureau of the Census.

TABLE 2
DISTRIBUTION OF TOTAL AND BLACK WORKERS, BY YEARS OF SCHOOL COMPLETED, 1990

Numbers in Thousands

YEARS OF SCHOOL	ALL WORKERS		BLACK WORKERS		
	number	percent distribution	number	percent distribution	percent of all workers
Total	117,914	100.00%	11,966	100.00%	10.15%
Less Than High School	17,922	15.20	2,381	19.90	13.29
High School	46,340	39.30	5,157	43.10	11.13
1-3 Years of College	25,353	21.50	2,669	22.30	10.53
4 Years of College or More	28,299	24.00	1,759	14.70	6.22

Source: Prepared by Brimmer & Company, Inc. Data from *Monthly Labor Review* November 1991.

TABLE 3
OCCUPATIONAL DISTRIBUTION OF EMPLOYMENT, BY RACE, 1990 AND 2005

Numbers in Thousands

OCCUPATION	ALL WORKERS				BLACK WORKERS					
	1990		2005		1990			2005		
	number	percent distribution	number	percent distribution	number	percent distribution	percent of all workers	number	percent distribution	percent of all workers
All Occupations	122,573	100.0%	147,191	100.0%	12,573	100.0%	10.0%	16,340	100.0%	11.1%
Executive, Administrative, Managerial	12,451	10.2	15,866	10.8	747	5.9	6.0	1,269	7.8	8.0
Professional Specialty	15,800	12.9	20,907	14.2	1,106	8.8	7.0	1,882	11.5	9.0
Technicians and Related	4,204	3.4	5,754	3.9	378	3.0	9.0	604	3.7	10.5
Marketing and Sales	14,088	11.5	17,489	11.9	845	6.7	6.0	1,259	7.7	7.2
Administrative Support, including Clerical	21,951	17.9	24,835	16.9	2,415	19.2	11.0	3,186	19.5	12.8
Service Occupations	19,204	15.7	24,806	16.9	3,265	26.0	17.0	3,857	23.6	16.0
Agricultural, Forestry, Fisheries	3,506	2.9	3,665	2.5	210	1.7	6.0	201	1.2	5.5
Precision Production and Craft	14,124	11.5	15,909	10.8	1,130	9.0	8.0	1,511	9.2	9.5
Operators, Fabricators, and Laborers	17,245	14.1	17,961	12.2	2,587	20.6	15.0	2,571	15.8	14.3

Source: Estimates for blacks prepared by Brimmer & Company, Inc. Data from *Monthly Labor Review*, November 1991.

TABLE 4
ESTIMATES AND PROJECTIONS OF THE U.S. POPULATION, CIVILIAN LABOR FORCE, EMPLOYMENT, AND MONEY INCOME, BY RACE, 1991–2000

Numbers in Thousands. Money Income in Millions of Dollars

	1991 number	percent	1992 number	percent	1993 number	percent	2000 number	percent
POPULATION								
Total	252,177	100.00%	254,922	100.00%	257,927	100.00%	274,815	100.00%
White	210,899	83.63	212,648	83.42	214,778	82.78	224,574	81.72
Black	31,164	12.36	31,673	12.42	32,137	12.62	35,525	12.93
Other Race	10,114	4.01	10,601	4.16	11,012	4.27	14,696	5.35
CIVILIAN LABOR FORCE								
Total	125,303	100.00	127,000	100.00	128,000	100.00	141,900	100.00
White	107,486	85.78	108,776	85.65	109,222	85.33	120,374	84.83
Black	13,542	10.81	13,780	10.85	14,080	11.00	15,893	11.20
Other Race	4,275	3.41	4,444	3.50	4,698	3.67	5,633	3.97
EMPLOYMENT								
Total	116,877	100.00	117,600	100.00	119,300	100.00	133,700	100.00
White	101,039	85.45	101,583	86.38	102,789	86.16	114,568	85.69
Black	11,863	10.15	11,960	10.17	12,192	10.22	13,985	10.46
Other Race	3,975	3.40	4,057	3.45	4,319	3.62	5,147	3.85
MONEY INCOME								
Total	$3,627,960	100.00	$3,761,200	100.00	$3,956,400	100.00	$5,725,668	100.00
White	3,228,041	88.98	3,347,468	89.00	3,517,240	88.90	5,055,765	88.30
Black	277,552	7.65	284,347	7.56	300,686	7.60	455,191	7.95
Other Race	122,367	3.37	129,385	3.44	138,474	3.50	214,712	3.75

Source: Estimates by Brimmer & Company, Inc. Data from U.S. Department of Commerce, Bureau of the Census, and U.S. Department of Labor, Bureau of Labor Statistics.

TABLE 5
BLACK MONEY INCOME DEFICIT, 1993 AND 2000

Amounts in Millions of Dollars

BENCHMARK	1993 PERCENT SHARE OF TOTAL INCOME	AMOUNT OF INCOME	DEFICIT amount	percent	2000 PERCENT SHARE OF TOTAL INCOME	AMOUNT OF INCOME	DEFICIT amount	percent	DEFICITS AS PERCENT OF GDP 1993	2000
Gross Domestic Product		$6,374,000				$8,942,000				
Money Income: Total		3,956,400				5,725,668				
Black Income										
Actual	7.60%	300,686			7.95%	455,191				
Parity										
Population	12.46	492,967	$-192,281	-39.10%	12.93	740,329	$-285,138	-38.52%	-3.02%	-3.19%
Civilian Labor Force	11.00	435,204	-134,518	-30.91	11.20	641,275	-186,084	-29.02	-2.11	-2.08
Employment	10.22	404,344	-103,658	-25.64	10.46	590,905	-135,714	-22.97	-1.63	-1.52

Source: Prepared by Brimmer & Company, Inc. Data from Table 4.

REFERENCES

Brimmer, Andrew F. 1966. "The Negro in the American Economy." Chapter 5 in *The American Negro Reference Book*, edited by John P. Davis. Englewood Cliffs, N.J.: Prentice-Hall.

Council of Economic Advisors. 1962. Press release dated September 25.

Monthly Labor Review. 1991. Vol. 114, No. 11.

U.S. Department of Commerce, Bureau of the Census. 1993. "Money Income of Households, Families, and Persons in the United States: 1992." *Current Population Reports*, Series P-60. Washington, D.C.: U.S. Government Printing Office.

U.S. Department of Commerce, Bureau of the Census. 1993. "Population Projections of the United States, by Age, Sex, Race, and Hispanic Origin: 1993 to 2050." *Current Population Reports*, Series P25-1104 (November). Washington, D.C.: U.S. Government Printing Office.

APPENDIX

TECHNIQUE FOR ESTIMATING THE COST OF RACIAL DISCRIMINATION

The first step in gauging the magnitude of the loss in Gross Domestic Product (GDP) because of discrimination against blacks was to estimate the gain that would occur if their present educational achievement were fully used. The question to be answered was: What would be the gain in GDP if blacks, with a given level of education, had the same average earnings as whites in the jobs which blacks actually hold? To make this estimate, data from the U.S. Census Bureau's *Current Population Reports* on "Money Income" were used.

Initially, for each age-sex-education group, the mean earnings of blacks were multiplied by the number of persons in each category and the results summed to produce the amount of money income received by blacks in a given year. This level was expressed as the *Base Case*.

Next, for each of the same age-sex-education categories, the mean earnings of blacks were changed to equal the mean earnings of whites. The multiplication and summation steps described above were repeated. These calculations produced *Adjusted Case I: Full Use of Present Education*. The resulting percentage increases in earnings for the years 1967, 1973, 1979, and 1993 are shown in Appendix Table A.1, Column (1).

In the second step, an estimate was made of the gain in income that might result if blacks' educational levels could be improved to the point where they equaled the levels achieved by whites and if blacks had the same mean earnings as whites at the same level of education. These calculations produced the percentage increases expressed as *Adjusted Case II: Full Use of Improved Education*, shown in Appendix Table A.1, Column (2).

The results of Adjusted Case I and Adjusted Case II were combined to produce *Adjusted Case III: Total Gain From Full Use of Improved Education (II) and Present Education (I)*, Shown in Appendix Table A.1, Column (3).

In the third step, the percentage increases in earnings were used to estimate gains in GDP. These are shown in Appendix Table A.2.

Initially, the wages and salaries component of GDP (including supplements) was raised by the percentage increases in total earnings brought over from Appendix Table A.1. The resulting gain in wages and salaries for Adjusted Case I is shown in Appendix Table A.2, Column (4). Next, the remaining component of GDP (equal to GDP minus the wages composition of employees) was derived. Column (6) for Case I shows the gain. Finally, the resulting combined increases in GDP for Case I are shown in Column (8). The same procedure was used to estimate the increase in GDP that might occur from full use of improved educational achievement by blacks—Adjusted Case II. The corresponding gains in this case are presented in Columns (10), (12), and (14).

The potential gain in GDP from the full use of blacks' present educational achievement and the full use of their improved education is shown in Case III, Columns (16), (18), and (20).

TABLE A1

GAINS IN EARNINGS FROM FULL USE OF PRESENT AND POTENTIAL EDUCATIONAL ACHIEVEMENT OF BLACKS IN THE UNITED STATES, 1967–93

Percentages

YEAR	ADJUSTED CASE I — FULL USE OF PRESENT EDUCATION	ADJUSTED CASE II — FULL USE OF IMPROVED EDUCATION	ADJUSTED CASE III — TOTAL GAIN FROM FULL USE OF IMPROVED EDUCATION (II) AND PRESENT EDUCATION (I)
1967	1.88%	1.72%	3.60%
1973	2.12	1.80	3.92
1979	2.30	1.92	4.22
1993	2.70	2.04	4.74

Source: Estimates prepared by Brimmer & Company, Inc. Data from U.S. Department of Commerce, Bureau of the Census.

TABLE A2
ESTIMATED GAIN IN GROSS DOMESTIC PRODUCT FROM FULL USE OF PRESENT AND POTENTIAL EDUCATIONAL ACHIEVEMENT OF BLACKS IN THE UNITED STATES, 1967–93

Amounts in Billions of Dollars

| | BASE LEVELS | | | ADJUSTED CASE I FULL USE OF PRESENT EDUCATION | | | | | |
| | GDP | COMP. OF EMPLOYEES | OTHER INCOME | INCREASE IN COMP. OF EMPLOYEES | | INCREASE IN OTHER INCOME | | TOTAL INCREASE IN GDP | |
YEAR	amount (1)	amount (2)	amount (3)	amount (4)	percent (5)	amount (6)	percent (7)	amount (8)	percent (9)
1967	$ 814.3	$ 475.5	$ 338.8	$ 8.9	1.88%	$ 3.2	0.94%	$ 12.1	1.49%
1973	1,349.8	812.8	537.0	17.2	2.12	5.7	1.06	22.9	1.70
1979	2,488.6	1,496.4	992.2	34.4	2.30	11.4	1.15	45.8	1.84
1993	6,374.0	3,781.1	2,592.9	102.1	2.70	35.0	1.35	137.1	2.15

Source: Prepared by Brimmer & Company, Inc. Data for GDP from the U.S. Department of Commerce, Bureau of Economic Analysis. Percentage increases in compensation and other income estimated by Brimmer & Company, Inc., based on data from the U.S. Department of Commerce, Bureau of the Census.

Continued

Table A2 Continued

ESTIMATED GAIN IN GROSS DOMESTIC PRODUCT FROM FULL USE OF PRESENT AND POTENTIAL EDUCATIONAL ACHIEVEMENT OF BLACKS IN THE UNITED STATES, 1967–93

Amounts in Billions of Dollars

| | ADJUSTED CASE II FULL USE OF IMPROVED EDUCATION | | | | | | ADJUSTED CASE III TOTAL GAIN FROM FULL USE OF IMPROVED EDUCATION (III) AND PRESENT EDUCATION (I) | | | | | |
| | INCREASE IN COMP. OF EMPLOYEES | | INCREASE IN OTHER INCOME | | TOTAL INCREASE IN GDP | | INCREASE IN COMP. OF EMPLOYEES | | INCREASE IN OTHER INCOME | | TOTAL INCREASE IN GDP | |
YEAR	amount (10)	percent (11)	amount (12)	percent (13)	amount (14)	percent (15)	amount (16)	percent (17)	amount (18)	percent (19)	amount (20)	percent (21)
1967	$ 8.2	1.72%	$ 2.9	0.86%	$ 11.1	1.36%	$ 17.1	3.60%	$ 6.1	1.80%	$ 23.2	2.85%
1973	14.6	1.80	4.8	0.90	19.4	1.43	31.8	3.91	10.5	1.96	42.3	3.13
1979	28.7	1.92	9.5	0.96	38.2	1.53	63.1	4.22	20.9	2.11	84.0	3.38
1993	77.1	2.04	26.4	1.02	103.5	1.62	179.2	4.74	61.5	2.37	240.7	3.78

Source: Prepared by Brimmer & Company, Inc. Data for GDP from the U.S. Department of Commerce, Bureau of Economic Analysis. Percentage increases in compensation and other income estimated by Brimmer & Company, Inc., based on data from the U.S. Department of Commerce, Bureau of the Census.

THE ECONOMIC COST
OF AFFIRMATIVE ACTION

Cecilia A. Conrad

THE ECONOMIC COST
OF AFFIRMATIVE ACTION

I n both the popular press and in scholarly journals, affirmative action's critics have recently become loud and vociferous. Mark Ahlseen in the August 1992 *Conservative Review* accuses affirmative action of having "a stifling effect on incentives and perceptions." In the July 5, 1993, issue of *National Review,* Lino Graglia describes affirmative action as a "fungus that can survive only underground in the dark." Especially damaging is the conclusion reached by Peter Brimelow and Leslie Spencer in the February 1993 issue of *Forbes.* Brimelow and Spencer claim that affirmative action has reduced the GNP of the United States by a whopping 4 percent! These statements appear in respected conservative publications and reflect the ideological slant of those journals. They are representative of statements from a growing number of critics who charge that government regulations of business are too costly for society. However, affirmative action's supporters have been largely silent on the question of its costs. In this information vacuum, specific numbers like the estimate by Brimelow and Spencer gain unwarranted credibility.

Its critics argue that affirmative action reduces economic efficiency in two ways: it forces firms to allocate resources to comply with regulations that yield little in the way of tangible benefits, and it forces employers to hire minority workers who are less qualified than the nonminority workers available for the same job. Not surprisingly, affirmative action's supporters offer a different analysis. They argue that without affirmative action an employer may pass over a qualified black worker for one who is less qualified but whose skin is white. Hence, affirmative action increases productivity by ensuring that the qualified black worker has an opportunity to compete for the job.

The author wishes to thank Alissia Gill for her research assistance.

33

The enforcement of equal employment opportunity law is a form of economic regulation and, like most regulatory activities, it imposes costs on society. The true extent of those costs lies at the center of the debate. This paper, which focuses on affirmative action in employment (not on set-aside programs, special incentive programs for minority businesses, or affirmative action in colleges and universities), finds that those costs are greatly exaggerated by opponents of affirmative action and other equal employment opportunity policies.

The following analysis answers the hyperbole of affirmative action's critics with a review of the previous research and with a multiple regression analysis of the link between productivity and workplace diversity. The dependent variable in the regression analysis is an index of labor productivity. The set of explanatory variables includes two indicators of the changing demographics of the workforce: the change in the female percentage and the change in the black percentage.

As my regression analysis will show, neither variable has a significant impact on productivity. The major costs of affirmative action are the costs of compliance, and those costs amount to roughly $2 billion a year—or less than one-half of one percent of GNP. These costs are not trivial, but they are probably small in comparison with the efficiency gains from full utilization of the skills of all Americans regardless of race or gender.

WHAT IS AFFIRMATIVE ACTION?

Affirmative action encompasses a wide array of activities designed to increase the number of women and minorities in the workforce and to improve their status. These activities range from the inclusion of the label "An Equal Employment Opportunity Employer" in job announcements to the preferential hiring of members of targeted groups. The typical affirmative action program involves an examination of a company's hiring practices in the past and the establishment of general goals for the future. Programs that give preferences to members of minority groups are rare.

Typically, employers develop affirmative action programs in response to the activities of either the Office of Federal Contract Compliance Programs (OFCCP) or of the Equal Employment Opportunity Commission (EEOC). The OFCCP oversees the enforcement of executive orders issued by the President of the United States prohibiting federal contractors from discriminating on the basis of race, religion, national origin or gender in employment decisions. While executive orders prohibiting employment discrimination by federal contractors date back to Franklin D. Roosevelt, Lyndon B. Johnson was the first President to impose a penalty on firms that failed to comply. Under Executive Order 11246, issued in 1965, federal contractors who fail to take affirmative action to end discrimination risk being barred from competition for future contracts. Federal contractors must submit plans to the OFCCP detailing specific goals and timetables for increasing the representation of women and minorities in their workforce.

Under the mandate of the Civil Rights Act of 1964, the EEOC requires all companies with more than 15 employees to submit yearly reports on workplace diversity. The commission has the authority to investigate charges of discrimination, file suits in federal court, and issue guidelines on employment discrimination. These guidelines typically call for the development of goals and timetables to increase the representation of women and minorities in the workforce. While these guidelines are not legally binding, the threat of litigation induces compliance. Affirmative action plans have also been required as an outcome of employment discrimination cases. The EEOC's 1973 negotiated settlement with American Telephone and Telegraph offers one prominent example.[1]

Affirmative action is not synonymous with quotas. Quotas, which require that a company hire or promote a fixed percentage of minorities and women, are explicitly prohibited by the Civil Rights Acts of 1964 and 1991. Furthermore, federal contractors routinely fall short of their affirmative action goals with no penalty imposed (Leonard 1985). Hence, the goals and timetables hardly constitute binding constraints on a firm's employment decisions. A firm can satisfy federal law without demonstrating any increase in the hiring of members of minority groups.

THE DIRECT COSTS OF AFFIRMATIVE ACTION

The direct costs of affirmative action programs include the costs of the administrative apparatus—EEOC and OFCCP budgets, the state and local agencies that enforce state laws, and so on. In addition, the direct costs include the costs to private industry of compliance with the guidelines established by these agencies.

In 1992, the EEOC had a budget of $212 million.[2] The OFCCP's 1992 budget was $55 million. The $267 million total omits spending by state and local agencies or by other federal agencies with authority to enforce equal employment opportunity provisions. Brimelow and Spencer estimate that these additional expenditures total $242 million.[3]

Less is known about the costs to private employers of compliance with EEOC and OFCCP regulations. There is a wide variance among the available estimates. At the upper end, a Business Roundtable study reported that 40 companies, primarily large firms, spent $217 million in 1971, an average cost per employee of $78 ($278 in 1992 dollars) (Leonard 1984). However, estimated costs ranged from $10 to $150 per employee (in 1971 dollars).

In their 1993 study, Brimelow and Spencer apply a rule of thumb of $20 million in compliance cost per $1 million spent on enforcement to arrive at an estimate of $6 billion in private compliance cost in 1992, or roughly $54 per worker (Brimelow and Spencer 1993). Their article represents the only recent attempt to quantify the impact of affirmative action on economic efficiency, but their analysis suffers from several damaging flaws. They derive their 4 percent of GNP estimate from a cost-of-regulation rule of thumb and from an ad hoc estimate of opportunity costs offered by an industrial psychologist. They double-count some costs and omit any references to statistical studies with contradictory findings. Most notably, they make no reference to the research of Jonathan Leonard, a respected economist at the University of California at Berkeley who has published more than a half-dozen articles on affirmative action in the top-ranked refereed journals of economics. Leonard's 1984 article in *The Journal of Human Resources* provides the foundation for the analysis which appears here.

The rule of thumb applied by Brimelow and Spencer represents an average cost of compliance with all regulatory activities, including regulations formulated by the Food and Drug Administration, the Environmental Protection Agency, and the Consumer Product Safety Commission. Installing scrubbers to reduce air pollution and conducting laboratory tests to establish the safety and efficacy of new drugs are both likely to be more costly activities than filing EEO reports.

Brimelow and Spencer credit John Hunter, an industrial psychologist, for the estimate that the inefficient allocation of workers because of affirmative action has reduced GNP by 2.5 percent. Hunter and a second industrial psychologist, Frank Schmidt, are staunch advocates of testing to screen workers and have long defended these tests from allegations that they unfairly discriminate against minority workers. Their estimate of 2.5 percent of GNP assumes that equal employment opportunity regulation has ended all employment testing. This assumption is false. Equal employment opportunity regulation does not prohibit testing; it requires that tests be job-related and fair. The 2.5 percent estimate also assumes that all employers who do not use employment tests omit them because of EEO regulation. However, there is no evidence offered regarding how many employers used tests prior to the implementation of these regulations.

At the other extreme are two 1981 studies of the costs of an affirmative action compliance review, also cited by Leonard (1984). One of these, a 1981 National Manufacturers' Association survey of 42 companies with an average workforce of 50,000, reported an average cost of $3,000 per firm or $1 per employee ($1.54 in 1992 dollars). The other study, for the U.S. Senate Labor Committee (under the chairmanship of Sen. Orrin Hatch), surveyed 245 contractors, each with an average workforce of 2,584 employees, and found an average cost of compliance of $24,000 per firm or roughly $8 per worker ($12.40 in 1992 dollars).

One difficulty with estimating the costs of compliance is identifying which expenditures are a direct response to EEOC or OFCCP regulations and which are expenditures that would have been made in the absence of these regulations. For example, a corporation's investment in a diversity training workshop for managers and supervisors may be in part motivated by the threat of a discrimination complaint, but it is also motivated by the reality of an increasingly diverse workforce. Flextime arrangements are used to recruit and retain women workers, but they are not technically part of an affirmative action program. Not all of the costs associated with workplace diversity represent costs of affirmative action.

My guess is that both the Business Roundtable estimate of $278 per employee and the Brimelow and Spencer estimate of $54 per employee probably overstate the costs of compliance. The Business Roundtable study was done in 1971. EEO regulations were still relatively new. There were costs to setting up the administrative systems to collect the information needed for reporting. Learning by doing and changes in technology are likely to have reduced the information costs since then.[4] In addition, within the study the estimated costs varied widely.

Some of the variance in these estimates might be due to economies of scale. The per-employee cost is lower for the companies included in the National Manufacturers' Association survey, whose average number of employees was over 50,000, than for the contractors included in the Congressional Labor Committee survey, whose average number of employees was less than 3,000.

The Center of American Business at Washington University, the source of the $20 million rule of thumb, estimates that the paperwork requirements of all regulatory activity totaled $20 billion per year. (Warren 1991) Assuming that the paperwork burden for equal employment opportunity regulation is proportional to its share of total federal spending on regulatory activities (roughly 3 percent), the paperwork burden imposed by equal employment opportunity regulation totals less than $1 billion annually or approximately $8.50 per worker.[5] This estimate is comparable to the $12.40 per employee figure (1992 dollars) reported by the Senate Labor Committee.

If we use the $12.40 estimate, we arrive at a total cost of compliance of approximately $1.4 billion. Add to this amount the cost of enforcement, estimated at roughly $509 million, and the estimated direct costs of equal employment opportunity policy total $1.9 billion a year.

AFFIRMATIVE ACTION AND PRODUCTIVITY: THE THEORY

One of the indirect costs (or benefits) of affirmative action is the impact it may have on productivity. Its opponents argue that affirmative action reduces productivity because it forces a firm to hire minorities and women who are less qualified than available white male workers. Affirmative action's supporters argue that without affirmative action an employer may pass over a qualified black worker for one who is less qualified but whose skin is white. Affirmative action can increase productivity by ensuring that the qualified black worker has an opportunity to compete for the job.

Affirmative action's opponents base much of their analysis on two assumptions: one, that affirmative action forces firms to hire a certain number or percentage of minority workers and two, that in a competitive labor market (without affirmative action), workers are allocated to jobs purely on merit. I have already addressed the first issue. There are certainly examples where employers have established quotas as part of their affirmative action programs, but they are neither legally required nor legally sanctioned. Furthermore, there is no evidence that quotas, where established, require a reduction in the standards for hiring workers. There is no evidence that employers, on a systematic basis, routinely hire blacks with lower qualifications than whites.

The second assumption, that labor markets are a meritocracy, requires a review of the theory of wage determination in competitive labor markets. A competitive labor market is one where there are many buyers and sellers—in other words, workers have a choice among many possible employers and employers have a choice among many possible workers. In a competitive labor market, information is available at low cost. Hence, workers are informed about wage offers and employers are informed about worker productivity. Transactions costs are low, workers are mobile, and employers have low fixed costs of hiring and firing workers.

In theory, competitive markets allocate workers to the jobs for which they are best suited. An employer will hire a worker as long as the marginal cost of that worker—his wage—is less than what the worker adds to the firm's revenues. In other words, an employer will hire a worker as long as hiring the worker increases profits. As long as a worker's skin color does not have any impact on his productivity, a profit maximizing firm has no incentive to engage in racial discrimination. A firm that did engage in racial discrimination could find itself at a cost disadvantage relative to a nondiscriminating firm. Hence, persistent differences in the wages and employment of black and white workers must reflect differences in the productivity of these workers. A quota, if it requires firms to hire less qualified workers, interferes with this market mechanism and leads to a misallocation of resources. Affirmative action without quotas reduces efficiency because resources are expended to end discrimination that, in theory, does not exist.

One problem with this analysis is that the underlying theoretical model of perfectly competitive labor markets oversimplifies how employment and wages are determined in the real world. In the real world, it may be difficult for an employer to evaluate fully a worker's skills prior to his employment. It may be costly to monitor his work effort following employment.

Discrimination: Theory and Evidence. In an environment where information is imperfect, employers may engage in statistical discrimination—relying on the real or perceived average characteristics of a group to evaluate the skills of an individual worker. George Akerlof (1984) presents a model of statistical discrimination. In Akerlof's model, there are two types of jobs. One job requires a worker to have obtained certain qualifications. The other job does not. The employer cannot observe directly whether an individual worker has the qualifications. To find out this information, the employer must test the worker at a nontrivial cost. Since it is not profit maximizing to test all workers, the employer must decide whom to test. If the employer believes that blacks or women are less likely to be qualified than whites, he will test a smaller proportion of those workers. Those qualified workers who are not tested will not be placed in jobs commensurate with their qualifications. They will earn the same pay that they would have earned without the qualifications. In the absence of a wage premium for acquiring skills, minority and women workers will have less incentive to acquire those skills. In the long run, the employer's perception that fewer minorities and women have the necessary qualifications may become a reality.

Akerlof's model, though highly stylized, captures a number of features of labor market discrimination. The test in Akerlof's model could either be a pre-employment written examination, a trial period of employment, or a period of employment at the lower rung of a job ladder before being allowed to move up. An employer who guesses that a small proportion of minority or female workers are qualified for the higher rung on the job ladder will be unwilling to test these workers. The employer will either not hire them or else hire them only for those unskilled jobs that offer little or no opportunity for advancement.

Affirmative action, in Akerlof's model, could ensure that tests are administered on the basis of criteria other than race. If more minority workers are tested, more of those with qualifications will be placed in jobs commensurate with their skills. With fewer underemployed workers, overall productivity should increase.

The other problem with the neoclassical theory of wage determination is that under the assumptions of the model, labor markets clear. Yet unemployment is a persistent feature of the macro-economy, and the unemployment rate for African Americans has exceeded 10 percent for the past decade. With unemployment, there can be a surplus of qualified workers. Employers can then use criteria other than merit in hiring workers with little effect on profits. In the jobs competition model popularized by Patrick Mason (1992) and William Darity and Rhonda Williams (1985), workers consolidate into groups on the basis of race, gender, or ethnicity to compete for a position in the job queue. The group that is first in line can limit the access of other groups by gaining control over training, evaluation, and job networks. With high unemployment and a surplus of qualified workers, affirmative action weakens the control of first movers over job access, but has little effect on productivity.

There is ample empirical evidence of both wage discrimination and of discrimination in employment opportunities. Econometric studies of the wage differences between black and white men consistently find a wage gap that cannot be explained by differences in skills. Conservatively, at least 30 percent of the wage gap between black and white men in the early 1970s was probably due to discrimination.[6] This differential is smaller today than 20 years ago, in part due to equal employment opportunity legislation.[7] Nevertheless, there is evidence that discrimination persists. The Urban Institute in the summer of 1990 conducted hiring audits in Washington, D.C., and in Chicago (Turner, Fix, and Struyk 1991). Ten pairs of young men—one black and one white—were carefully matched on all characteristics that could affect a hiring decision. They applied for entry level jobs advertised in newspapers. In 20 percent of the cases, the white tester advanced farther in the hiring process. In 15 percent of the cases only the white received a job offer. The black tester advanced farther than the white in only 7 percent of the cases and received a job offer, while the white partner did not receive an offer in only 5 percent of the audits.

If there is discrimination in labor markets, then affirmative action, to the extent that it eliminates this discrimination, has the potential to increase overall productivity. Andrew Brimmer, a former member of the Federal Reserve Board of Governors, estimates that if the U.S. economy fully utilized the existing human capital stock of African Americans, GNP would increase by 2.15 percentage points (Brimmer 1995).

To what extent does affirmative action help to end discrimination? Studies comparing the performance of federal contractors with noncontractors suggest that the affirmative action requirements imposed on contractors have increased their employment of African Americans and have increased their representation in skilled blue collar work and in managerial and professional occupations[8] (Leonard 1990). Perhaps the most persuasive evidence is offered by a case study of the South Carolina textile industry by James Heckman and Brook Payner (1989). They find that despite an available pool of qualified black workers prior to the 1965 Executive Order, blacks were underrepresented in this industry. Following the Executive Order and under EEOC pressure, the number of blacks employed *grew* dramatically. While it is impossible to determine conclusively if the wage gains enjoyed by blacks of either sex since the 1960s would have occurred without the Civil Rights Act of 1964, the timing of these gains appears more than coincidental.

Even if affirmative action eliminates some discrimination, it can have a negative effect on productivity if litigation-shy employers hire less qualified workers or if the increased diversity of the workforce leads to conflict on the shop floor. Economist Gary Becker (1971) has developed a model of what happens when workers have a taste for discrimination. His model predicts that employers will segregate workers from different groups to minimize worker conflict. Since equal employment opportunity law is unlikely to permit this physical separation of workers, the decrease in work effort by white (or male) workers unhappy working with blacks (or women) could reduce productivity.

AFFIRMATIVE ACTION AND PRODUCTIVITY: THE EVIDENCE

Despite the frequency of the complaint that affirmative action programs reduce productivity, there have been very few attempts to test this hypothesis directly. I have identified three. Two are case studies of specific occupations or industries. One of these case studies, by Nolan Penn, Percy Russell, and Harold Simon (1986), compares the activities of medical school graduates, some of whom had been admitted to medical school under special admissions programs. One of the expressed goals of this affirmative action program was to increase the supply of physicians to underserved communities. Penn *et al.* find that the doctors who had been admitted through special admissions saw more patients per day, were more likely to service inner city and rural communities, and had more patients from low-status socioeconomic groups. Brent Steel and Nicholas Lovrich (1987) evaluate the impact of affirmative action programs on the performance of police departments. They study the effect of increases in the utilization of women officers on three indicators of police department performance—per capita crime rates, clearance rates (crimes solved), and expenditures. Departments with activist affirmative action policies appear no more or less able to counter the trend in rising crime rates. There were no differences in the costs of operation and no differences in the ability to solve crimes. Neither of these studies examines the effect of affirmative action on private employers.

Jonathan Leonard (1984) in an article in the *Journal of Human Resources* addresses both questions concerning affirmative action programs and productivity in the private sector, namely, whether these programs have led to the hiring of less productive workers and whether they have reduced overall productivity. To answer the first question, he estimates changes over time in the ratio of minority-to-white and female-to-male productivity. In theory, if affirmative action has led to the hiring of less qualified workers, these ratios would decline. Leonard finds that between 1966 and 1977, the employment of women and minorities increased and this increase in employment was accompanied by an increase in their relative marginal productivities. Leonard concludes that there is no evidence of reverse discrimination or of a significant decline in the relative productivity of minorities or females.

Leonard also directly tests the hypothesis that increases in minority and female employment have decreased overall productivity. Using state-level data on net output by industry, Leonard estimates the impact on net worth (in 1977) of changes in the percentage of the minority and female labor force between 1966 and 1977. Controls were included for region and industry, for capital stock, and for the percentage of the industry that was blue-collar. Neither the change in the minority percentage nor the change in the female percentage had a significant impact on industry productivity.

Leonard's study focused on the period between 1966 and 1977. Some would argue that affirmative action's negative effect on productivity becomes more pronounced in the longer run as firms exhaust the supply of qualified minority and female workers. Furthermore, Leonard focused exclusively on manufacturing industries. Over the 1980s, the share of total employment in manufacturing has declined. What has been the impact of affirmative action on other sectors of the economy?

Affirmative Action and Productivity in the 1980s. My own regression analysis (see Appendix) examines the relationship between productivity and changes in black and female employment shares between 1984 and 1988.[9] The analysis finds that industry productivity is affected by the change in capital stock, time, and the industry category. Productivity is lower in services, manufacturing, and retail trade as compared with mining, transportation and communications, and finance, insurance and real estate (F.I.R.E.). Growth in the capital stock tends to increase productivity, and productivity tends to increase over time.

Neither of the indicators of workplace diversity appears to affect productivity. (The coefficients on the change in the black share of employment and the female share of employment are not significantly different from zero.) Like Leonard, I find no evidence that changes in the shares of employment of these two groups affect productivity.

Admittedly, this approach has important limitations. The period 1983 to 1988 is generally regarded as one in which equal employment opportunity laws were not actively enforced. Indeed, the black share of total employment in nonagricultural industries was relatively constant over this period, with the exception of transportation and communications. Women's share of total employment was also relatively constant. Furthermore, both my analysis and Leonard's examine the effect of changes in the employment shares of minorities and women on productivity. Yet the observed changes in employment shares might not be the result of the enforcement of EEO laws. If the laws are not enforced, we would expect to see no effect on productivity. Hence, my findings have two possible interpretations: (1) the laws were enforced but had no effect on productivity, or (2) the laws were not enforced. However, if the laws were not enforced, it is difficult to justify the claim that affirmative action has had large negative effects.

A second limitation of this analysis is that the level of aggregation conceals shifts in employment between firms and the associated changes in productivity. However, if affirmative action has had as large an impact as some of its critics allege, we would expect to see some evidence in aggregate indicators of productivity.

Given these limitations, it is helpful to study two specific industries with a history of active EEO law enforcement. This analysis yields mixed results. Heckman and Payner (1989) offer persuasive evidence that affirmative action programs increased black employment in textiles. Productivity in textiles grew at a lower pace than in other nondurables. American Telephone and Telegraph, a major competitor in telecommunications, was required to implement an affirmative action program as part of its historic agreement with the EEOC. Productivity in telecommunications grew faster than productivity in other industries in the same category.

There is no conclusive evidence that affirmative action programs have reduced productivity. There are undeniably instances in which a black worker with less qualifications is hired in preference to a white. However, the Urban Institute study suggests these instances are far less prevalent than is widely perceived. These cases of reverse discrimination are probably more than counterbalanced by the cases where a more qualified black is hired who would not have been hired in the absence of affirmative action.

AFFIRMATIVE ACTION AND NEGATIVE STEREOTYPES

Some critics of affirmative action accept that there is discrimination in labor markets, but argue that affirmative action makes a bad situation worse. Their basic concern is the stigma that affirmative action may impose on members of targeted groups. This stigma is created by the perception that members of targeted groups would not qualify for employment in the absence of affirmative action programs.

Several studies by industrial psychologists confirm that there is a negative stigma associated with affirmative action programs. Madeline Heilman, Caryn Block, and Jonathan Lucas (1992) asked study participants to rate the qualifications of recent hires at a hypothetical firm. In some cases, participants were informed that the employer had an active affirmative action program. In those cases, participants gave a lower rating to the female job candidates than in the cases where they were not given this information. Luis Garcia, Nancy Erskine, Kathy Hawn, and Susanne Casmay (1981) report similar results in a study of minority applicants to a hypothetical university.

Stephen Coates and Glenn Loury (1993) take this argument one step further. They argue that with affirmative action, an employer's negative stereotype may become a self-fulfilling prophecy. In their theoretical model, a firm engaged in statistical discrimination is forced to hire workers under an affirmative action program. Initially, black and white workers are equally productive, but an employer perceives, incorrectly, that blacks are less qualified than whites, and therefore lowers the standards to increase the number of blacks hired. Once the standards for blacks are lowered, blacks have less incentive to meet the "white standard," so over time, depending on the parameters of the model, blacks may become less qualified than whites. The employer's negative stereotype is then reinforced.

But the evidence does not bear out the Coates and Loury scenario of lowered skills. James Heckman and Brook Payner (1989) find that the average level of educational attainment increased among black South Carolinians even as their employment opportunities in textiles increased. Most colleges and universities have some sort of affirmative action program in admissions, yet Scholastic Aptitude Test scores for blacks have improved relative to whites, and scores for women have improved relative to those for men.[10] The credentials offered to colleges and universities and to employers appear to be stronger today than 20 years ago despite 20 years of affirmative action.

CONCLUSIONS

Affirmative action policies clearly impose some costs on society. These costs include the costs of the regulatory apparatus—EEOC and OFCCP budgets—and the costs to employers of compliance with the regulations these federal offices promulgate. I estimate the total costs at just under $2 billion a year. In addition, if affirmative action creates the image that minority workers are less qualified than their nonminority counterparts, it may impose psychological costs on its beneficiaries, although this burden may be no greater than that borne by qualified minorities unable to get a job in the absence of affirmative action.

However, a reduction in productivity does not appear to be a major cost of affirmative action policies. In theory, worker productivity could be reduced if employers, in an effort to avoid litigation, hire minority workers with less ability to do the job than that of white job candidates.

Productivity could also be affected by a reduction of worker effort due to conflict on the shop floor or disgruntlement of white workers. Productivity could be reduced by the abandonment of employment tests or screens perceived as racially biased. Anecdotal evidence suggests that, in individual cases, affirmative action has had all of these effects and more. Yet, there is no evidence that the overall impact of affirmative action has been negative. There is no smoking gun. The cases where affirmative action results in the hiring of a less qualified worker appear to be dwarfed by the cases where affirmative action results in the hiring of a worker on merit rather than the color of his or her skin.

NOTES

1. See *EEOC* v. *American Telephone & Telegraph Co.,* 556 F. 2d 167 (3rd Circuit, 1977), cert. denied sub nom. *Communications Workers of America* v. *EEOC,* 438 US 915 (1978). The EEOC alleged that AT&T's employment policies discriminated against both women and minorities. As part of the settlement, AT&T agreed to pay more than $31 million in back pay to affected employees and agreed to implement a comprehensive affirmative action plan. AT&T began to actively recruit women into nontraditional careers (including telephone repair and line work), set up scholarships to train more women and minorities in science and engineering, and set goals and timetables to recruit and promote more women and minorities into management positions.

2. Not all of this budget was devoted to ending discrimination on the basis of race and sex. The EEOC is also charged with enforcement of laws prohibiting discrimination on the basis of disability or age. Unfortunately, a breakdown of the EEOC's budget by type of discrimination is not available.

3. I exclude from their estimate the expenditure by the Department of Education which is primarily directed at higher education. There is also potentially some double-counting of funds in their estimates. EEOC's budget total includes grants to state and local governments.

4. The most recent survey of compliance costs is the 1981 congressional study cited by Jonathan Leonard (1984).

5. This calculation is based on 115 million total employed in the nonagricultural workforce.

6. A summary of the empirical evidence is available in a standard textbook in labor economics, *Modern Labor Economics: Theory and Public Policy,* by Ronald G. Ehrenberg and Robert S. Smith (1987). Ehrenberg and Smith conclude that between 15 and 50 percent of the earnings differential between blacks and whites may be due to discrimination (p. 537).

   Different studies obtain different results, depending on the data set and on the variables included in the analysis. It is noteworthy that even in an occupation which blacks appear to dominate, professional basketball, there is evidence of discrimination. Lawrence Kahn and Peter Sherer (1988) find that after controlling for productivity and market-related variables, professional basketball players who are black earn 20 percent less than the ones who are white.

7. Research using data from the 1980s, cited by Ronald Ehrenberg and Robert Smith, found that less than 17 percent of the earnings differential between black and white males could be attributed to discrimination (Ehrenberg and Smith 1987, 537).

   A more recent study by June O'Neill found that virtually all of the wage gap between young black males and young white males could be explained by differences in characteristics (O'Neill 1990). However, the O'Neill study includes scores on the Armed Forces Qualifying Test (AFQT) as an explanatory variable. To the extent that scores on the AFQT correlate with race more than with ability, the coefficient on this test score will reflect racial discrimination in wages. With the AFQT score omitted from her analysis, O'Neill estimates that differences in productivity-related characteristics explain 85 percent of the earnings differential. In other words, roughly 15 percent of the differential could be due to discrimination.

8. There is little evidence that the contract compliance program has improved the employment prospects of white women (Leonard 1989).

9. The dependent variable is the index of productivity for each industry in the years 1984-88. The measure of productivity is an index of output per man hour constructed by the Bureau of Labor Statistics. The base year for this index is 1982. I matched this data with employment share data from *Employment and Earnings* and with measures of capital stock (primarily at the 2-digit SIC code) from *Fixed Reproducible Tangible Wealth in the United States, 1925-89.* The sample consists of 57 industries (primarily at the 3-digit SIC code level of aggregation) with information available from both sources over the entire period, 1983-88. Included as explanatory variables are total employment in the industry, the change in net capital stock, the change in the share of the workforce that is female, the change in the share of the workforce that is black, and controls for year of observation and for industry category. This sample includes the retail trade; transportation and communications; manufacturing; mining; and finance, insurance and real estate (F.I.R.E.) industries.

10. The average score on the verbal section of the Scholastic Aptitude Test (SAT) for blacks increased by 19 points between 1976 and 1991, and the score on the math section increased by 31 points. In comparison, the average verbal score for whites fell by 10 points and the average math score fell by 4 points (Horton and Smith 1993). There is also a narrowing of the gender gap on the SAT once adjustments are made for differences in the population of test takers (Murphy 1992).

REFERENCES

Akerlof, George. 1984. *An Economic Theorist's Book of Tales.* Chicago: University of Chicago Press.

Ahlseen, Mark. 1992. "The Economics of Affirmative Action." *Conservative Review,* Vol. 3, August.

Becker, Gary. 1971. *The Economics of Discrimination.* Chicago: University of Chicago Press.

Belz, Herman. 1990. *Equality Transformed: A Quarter Century of Affirmative Action.* New Brunswick, N.J.: Transaction Publishers.

Brimelow, Peter, and Leslie Spencer. 1993. "When Quotas Replace Merit, Everybody Suffers." *Forbes,* February 15.

Brimmer, Andrew. 1995. "The Economic Cost of Discrimination." (In this volume.)

Coates, Stephen, and Glenn Loury. 1993. "Will Affirmative-Action Policies Eliminate Negative Stereotypes?" *American Economic Review,* Vol. 83, No. 4.

Darity, William, and Williams, Rhonda. 1985. "Peddlers Forever? Culture, Competition and Discrimination." *American Economic Review,* Vol. 75, No. 2.

Ehrenberg, Ronald G., and Robert S. Smith. 1987. *Modern Labor Economics: Theory and Public Policy.* Glenview, IL: Scott, Foresman and Company.

Garcia, Luis T., Nancy Erskine, Kathy Hawn, and Susanne P. Casmay. 1981. "The Effect of Affirmative Action on Attributions About Minority Group Members." *Journal of Personality,* Vol. 49, No. 4.

Graglia, Lino A. 1993. "Beyond Racism: Affirmative Action," *National Review,* July 5.

Heckman, James J., and Brook S. Payner. 1989. "Determining the Impact of Federal Antidiscrimination Policy on the Economic Status of Blacks: A Study of South Carolina." *American Economic Review,* Vol. 79, No. 1.

Heilman, Madeline E., Caryn J. Block, and Jonathan A. Lucas. 1992. "Presumed Incompetent? Stigmatization and Affirmative Action Efforts." *Journal of Applied Psychology,* Vol. 77, No. 4.

Horton, Carrell Peterson, and Jessie Carney Smith. 1993. *The Statistical Record of Black America.* Detroit: Gale Research Inc.

Kahn, Lawrence M., and Peter D. Sherer. 1988. "Racial Differences in Professional Basketball Players' Compensation." *Journal of Labor Economics,* Vol. 6, No. 1.

Leonard, Jonathan S. 1984. "Anti-Discrimination or Reverse Discrimination: The Impact of Changing Demographics, Title VII and Affirmative Action on Productivity." *Journal of Human Resources,* Vol. 19, No. 2.

—————. 1985. "What Promises Are Worth: The Impact of Affirmative Action Goals." *Journal of Human Resources,* Vol. 20, No. 1.

—————. 1989. "Women and Affirmative Action." *Journal of Economic Perspectives,* Vol. 3, No. 1.

—————. 1990. "The Impact of Affirmative Action Regulation and Equal Employment Law on Black Employment." *Journal of Economic Perspectives,* Vol. 4, No. 4.

Mason, Patrick. 1992. "The Divide-and-Conquer and Employer/Employee Models of Discrimination: Neoclassical Competition as a Familial Defect." *The Review of Black Political Economy,* Vol. 20, No. 4.

Murphy, Susan H. 1992. "Closing the Gender Gap: What's Behind the Difference in Test Scores, What Can Be Done About It." *The College Board Review,* No. 163, Spring.

O'Neill, June. 1990. "The Role of Human Capital in Earnings Differences Between Black and White Men." *Journal of Economic Perspectives,* Vol. 4, No. 4.

Penn, Nolan E., Percy J. Russell, and Harold J. Simon. 1986. "Affirmative Action at Work: A Survey of Graduates of the University of California, San Diego, Medical School." *American Journal of Public Health,* Vol. 76, No. 9.

Steel, Brent S., and Nicholas P. Lovrich. 1987. "Equality and Efficiency Tradeoffs in Affirmative Action—Real or Imagined? The Case of Women in Policing." *Social Science Journal,* Vol. 24, No. 1.

Turner, Margery, Michael Fix, and Raymond J. Struyk. 1991. *Opportunities Denied, Opportunities Diminished: Racial Discrimination in Hiring.* Washington, DC: The Urban Institute Press.

Warren, Melinda. 1991. *Government Regulation and American Business.* St. Louis, Mo.: Center for the Study of American Business.

APPENDIX TABLE: STATISTICAL METHODOLOGY

VARIABLE NAME	DEFINITION	SAMPLE MEANS	COEFFICIENT (t-statistic in parentheses)
Total Employment	Total number of workers employed in industry category	582,365	-0.001 (-1.192)
Capital	Proportionate change in net capital stock (2-digit SIC code)	0.020	50.908 (2.199)
Time — Trend Variable	1984=1, 1985=2, 1986=3, 1987=4, 1988=5		3.451 (5.930)
Services*	=1 if service industry, 0= otherwise	0.070	-24.942 (-5.489)
Manufacturing*	=1 if manufacturing industry, 0= otherwise	0.509	-11.379 (-3.323)
Retail*	=1 if retail, =0 otherwise	0.263	-18.910 (-5.015)
Transportation*	=1 if transportation or communications industry, 0= otherwise	0.088	-5.444 (-1.245)
FIRE*	=1 if finance, insurance or real estate industry, =0 otherwise	0.018	-6.369 (-0.873)
FSHR	Change in the ratio — women employees/total employees	0.154	0.467 (1.378)
BSHR	Change in ratio — black employees/ total employees	0.204	0.647 (1.545)
Sample Size			263
Adjusted R Squared			0.324

* Omitted industry is mining. Sample did not include wholesale trade and construction.

THE EFFECTIVENESS OF EQUAL EMPLOYMENT OPPORTUNITY POLICIES

M.V. Lee Badgett

and

Heidi I. Hartmann

THE EFFECTIVENESS OF EQUAL EMPLOYMENT OPPORTUNITY POLICIES

A
lthough issues related to the civil rights of women and people of color have concerned decision makers in the United States for over 200 years, federal policy did not clearly codify a principle of equal employment opportunity until the passage of the Civil Rights Act of 1964. Title VII of this act specifically forbade employers to discriminate against individuals because of their race, color, religion, sex, or national origin in decisions regarding hiring, firing, compensation, or other terms of employment. President Johnson's 1965 Executive Order 11246 went further to require federal contractors to take affirmative action to remove discriminatory practices. The existence of an official policy does not, however, ensure its effectiveness. This report focuses on the effects of federal equal employment opportunity (EEO) policies, including affirmative action, on two overlapping groups, African Americans and women, by reviewing econometric evidence of the effects of policy on labor market outcomes, particularly wages and employment.[1] In the few cases in which studies have also examined other racial or ethnic groups, those results are also included.

Many other surveys of the econometric literature have been written by economists actively engaged in this research (see Table 1). Conducted at different stages of the research in this area and at different stages of policy structure and enforcement, these surveys reach moderately different conclusions about the effectiveness of federal EEO efforts but often raise issues addressed in later research. In addition to reviewing much of the same literature, this report attempts to match criticisms to responses, interpretations to reinterpretations, and new answers to old questions in an effort to identify what we know about the effects of federal EEO policy. This report also considers these studies in a broader context than some other surveys, both with respect to groups covered (e.g., John H. Donohue and James Heckman's focus on men [1991]) and to the questions that need to be answered (e.g., the effect of institutions).

Uncertainty in results and ambiguity in interpretation characterize much of this research literature. The uncertainty stems partly from the imperfections of available data and the need to patch together variables to measure enforcement or policy change. We have detailed personal, income, and employment data on representative samples of individuals from the monthly Current Population Survey (CPS) and the decennial census but know virtually nothing about individuals' employers; we have unrepresentative employer-level data from EEO-1 forms with little information about the firm and its employees beyond totals by race, sex, and occupation. This report reviews the major quantitative studies that have pieced data together to measure the effects of policy using some direct policy measurement, such as Equal Employment Opportunity Commission (EEOC) expenditures or the presence of a government contract. And although case studies often provide more subtle detail on the impact of EEO policies, studies of one or only a few employers may not be representative of the average employer's response. Those studies, therefore, are not included in this report.

The remainder of this study is divided into 10 sections. The first section previews its basic findings. The second section reviews federal policy and legal requirements for firms. The third section reviews the economic models that drive research methodology and hypotheses. The fourth and fifth sections review the literature on Title VII, while the sixth covers EEOC class-action suits. The seventh and eighth sections cover the federal contractor compliance program. In some cases, studies combine the effects of Title VII and the contractor requirements, and those studies are classified according to the emphasis on one or the other. The ninth section discusses two papers that examine how EEO programs affect firms' performance and profits. The final section suggests questions for further research.

PREVIEW OF FINDINGS

Although statistical studies usually leave room for doubt, both in interpretation and even in the results, this report finds some clear patterns in the empirical economic literature. At the broadest level, measures of activity related to both Title VII and the federal contract compliance programs are consistently correlated with labor market outcomes (e.g., wages, employment, occupational status, and quits) after removing the effect of other labor market influences. In most cases, these effects are consistent with the policies' intended outcomes, i.e., the improvement of wages and employment among people of color and white women, with improvement usually measured relative to the effects on white men.

The effects of Title VII variables are small and not always statistically significant, but the measurements of enforcement pressure are not precise and are applied at highly aggregated levels. That variations in these imprecise policy measures can help explain wages or employment at such aggregate levels supports the belief that the effects of equal employment opportunity policy are indeed widespread and significant.

The effects of the federal contract compliance program are also small and subject to different interpretations. Putting the evidence of wage and employment effects together, however, suggests that the affirmative action requirement has led to an increase in demand, most clearly for black men and black women. In the 1970s, gains were made across the range of occupations. Other doubts about the demand-shift interpretation arising from concerns about data and contractor selection actually push in the other direction, i.e., toward the possibility that noncontractor firms also reduced discrimination so that the measured contractor impact is a *conservative* measure of policy effects. These employment effects persist until the 1980s. The timing of this reversal of contractor effects coincides with a dramatic shift in the enforcement philosophy under President Reagan, providing further evidence that policy affects employer behavior.

Bits and pieces of evidence show that the effects of these policies have not come at the expense of either competitiveness or fairness of employment practices. Looking at a large sample of closely monitored firms reveals no pattern of strict adherence to goals in a way that would suggest the enforcement of quotas. In practice, affirmative action appears to mean greater efforts in hiring protected groups in growing firms without sacrificing quality.

EEO AND AFFIRMATIVE ACTION LEGAL REQUIREMENTS

The legal history of affirmative action involves legislation, presidential orders, and court decisions that together have defined EEO and affirmative action requirements. Antidiscrimination policies developed teeth in the 1960s when legal sanctions and institutionalized enforcement agencies were developed to back up the policy goals. Since 1964, the various agencies and guidelines that originally directed the federal government's antidiscrimination efforts have been condensed and combined into two agencies, the Office of Federal Contract Compliance Programs (OFCCP) and the EEOC, with the Department of Justice taking the responsibility for enforcing Title VII for nonfederal public employers.

Johnson's 1965 Executive Order 11246 extended previous presidential directives against employment discrimination by establishing the Office of Federal Contract Compliance. The order required the following of federal contractors with 50 or more employees and contracts over $50,000:

> ... take affirmative action to ensure that applicants are employed, and that employees are treated during employment, without regard to their race, creed, color, or national origin. Such action shall include, but not be limited to the following: employment, upgrading, demotion, or transfer; recruitment or recruitment advertising; layoff or termination; rates of pay or other forms of compensation; and selection for training, including apprenticeship.

The order was amended to include gender in 1967. The various enforcement agencies from different departments were consolidated in 1979 into the OFCCP within the Department of Labor. The OFCCP now enforces the rules for all federal contractors; sanctions include cancellation of contracts, debarment from future contracts, and recommendations that the EEOC take further legal action.

Title VII. Title VII of the Civil Rights Act of 1964, which prohibits employment discrimination, applies to private firms with 15 or more employees, educational institutions, state and local governments, employment agencies, and unions. The EEOC enforces Title VII through conciliation, if possible, or through the courts, if necessary. In amendments to the Civil Rights Act in 1972, the EEOC was given the authority to initiate lawsuits.

In practice, Title VII allows but does not require affirmative action programs unless court-imposed after a finding of discrimination. The EEOC encourages firms to develop voluntary affirmative action plans. The EEOC also cooperates with state and local agencies set up to enforce state and local equal employment opportunity laws. All firms with 100 or more employees must file annual EEO-1 reports on the race and gender composition of their workforce.

The Role of the Courts. The judicial branch of government has interpreted and enforced the requirements set up by Congress, presidents, and the enforcement agencies. Court decisions also set up a feedback mechanism whereby judicial interpretations are incorporated in new legislation and agency guidelines.

Definitions of illegal discrimination come from judicial interpretations. This includes the removal of overtly discriminatory practices that result in "disparate treatment" of individuals because of their race, color, religion, sex, or national origin. One exception allows discrimination by sex if sex is a "bona fide occupational qualification," that is, "reasonably necessary to the normal operation of that particular business or enterprise." Discrimination also includes other aspects of employment systems that appear to be neutral with regard to different groups of workers but in fact result in an "adverse impact" on minorities or women. The criterion for judging whether this sort of discrimination has taken place is the outcome—the result of a firm's practices, not simply its intent. These practices are not always illegal, however. Practices having an adverse impact may be allowed if firms can prove that they serve a "business necessity." This exception will be discussed further below.

Affirmative Action Plans. In principle, affirmative action is concerned with active removal of all possible discriminatory practices. In practice, the formal policy requirements vary, depending on the source of the affirmative action plan. An affirmative action plan for federal contractors formally requires them to find and correct employment practices that have an adverse impact. This includes self-analysis of the effects of their employment practices as well as monitoring to evaluate the plan's results, particularly with respect to statistics about its workforce and the local labor force.

Self-analysis by firms and evaluation by the EEOC and OFCCP are guided by the development of case law and administrative guidelines that constitute a set of quasi-regulations regarding employment decisions, including selection, promotion, and compensation decisions. No clear set of actual regulations exists for employers to follow, and even the generally accepted practices and administrative guidelines cannot be considered as fixed rules.[2]

Some of the basic criteria enabling employers to detect and avoid the subtler form of discrimination, that which results in "adverse impact," have been incorporated into the Uniform Guidelines on Employee Selection Procedures used by both the EEOC and OFCCP in monitoring and enforcement. (A series of Supreme Court decisions in 1989 threatened to change these substantially, but the 1991 Civil Rights Act restored most of the old principles.) Establishing goals and timetables provides a target for firms and a means of judging progress. The OFCCP may evaluate a contractor's affirmative action plan and its results, as well as actual employment practices, in a compliance review.

Voluntary plans vary in their form and ambition (as do contract-required plans in practice), but the most rigorous plans resemble the kind enforced by the OFCCP. Noncontractor firms that have not had an externally imposed affirmative action plan have only the monitoring requirement mentioned earlier. The two main elements of a voluntary or federal contractor affirmative action plan, self-analysis and correction, may be supplemented when a plan is court-ordered after a finding of discrimination or is agreed to in conciliation of complaints. Within the context of this sort of plan, the general goal of eliminating discriminatory practices is the same. But in this case, remedies such as hiring quotas, back pay, and legal costs may be imposed (Schlei and Grossman 1983).

The changing basic structure of requirements provides one way that studies can attempt to measure variations in the effect of EEO policies over time, especially with respect to the 1972 amendments to the Civil Rights Act. The other sort of "natural experiment" concerns the quantity and quality of actions by the enforcement agencies. Jonathan Leonard (1989 and 1990) reviews the history of EEO enforcement and concludes that, although effort and effectiveness increased in the 1970s, the overall effort was not large.

The Decline of Federal Enforcement in the 1980s. The most notable shift in enforcement occurred with the Reagan administration's attempts to revise formal policies radically, even though these efforts had a limited impact on EEOC and OFCCP guidelines. The philosophical and formal base of affirmative action in employment remained relatively intact despite the many statements by presidential appointees challenging the validity of the enterprise. Surprisingly, despite pressure from inside and outside his administration, Reagan never rescinded Johnson's executive order.

The day-to-day enforcement of the rules and guidelines clearly changed during the Reagan years. Severe budget cuts caused a significant OFCCP personnel reduction of more than 50 percent between 1979 and 1985 (DuRivage 1985). Although the number of compliance reviews increased during the same period, other indicators of OFCCP vigilance, such as the number and amount of back pay awards, show a marked decline. During the first six years of the Reagan administration, only two contractors were debarred from bidding on a federal contract, compared to thirteen such debarments during Carter's four-year term. Informal policy changes ended contractor requirements for multiyear goals and timetables and left only one-year goals.[3]

EEOC shifted its focus to cases involving individuals rather than companies or industries (Burbridge 1986). In the first few Reagan years, fewer discrimination charges resulted in settlements or litigation, and more cases were determined "no cause." Some significant but informal rule changes did occur; for example, during a brief period field agents received oral instructions not to include goals and timetables in consent decrees or settlement agreements. Thus, the periods of agency enforcement and legal authority activity can be roughly divided into 1964 to 1972, 1972 to 1980, and post-1980.

ECONOMIC THEORIES OF DISCRIMINATION

Since the 1957 publication of Gary S. Becker's *The Economics of Discrimination,* economists have been developing and refining theories of employment discrimination. The proliferation of theories stems from academic processing as well as the need to understand the basis of discrimination in order to design appropriate policies. This proliferation has occurred mainly with respect to theories of race and, to a lesser extent, with gender. In this section, we will not review and critique all such theories,[4] but rather will fit the theories used in the empirical literature into a general framework. This is a relatively straightforward task; although the theories tend to be elaborate, the data available for empirical work allow only rough approximations of tests suggested by such theories.

The Neoclassical Model. Most economists conducting these studies base their work on the mainstream or "neoclassical" model, which treats labor like any commodity bought and sold in a market, with wages serving as its price. In the simplest neoclassical model, a firm makes employment decisions in a way that maximizes the firm's profits (revenues minus costs): if hiring an additional worker increases profits, the firm will hire the worker. As long as the extra revenue brought in from selling what the worker produces is greater than the wage paid to the worker, the firm's profits will increase by hiring more labor.

As hiring increases, two conflicting forces push the market wage toward a stable level, or equilibrium: (1) inducing qualified workers to work more hours requires higher wages, generating a supply curve, and (2) increasing employment reduces each new worker's productivity while other production factors, such as equipment, do not increase right away, generating a demand curve. At this equilibrium, each worker is paid the amount that he or she contributes to the firm's revenue, i.e., according to her productivity. Each person who wants a job will end up with the job that represents her best position in the labor market.[5]

In this general model, differences in wages and employment levels by race or gender will be generated by differences either in labor supply (reflecting workers' choices of work hours and acquisition of skills that generally increase productivity) or labor demand (reflecting the productivity of the firm's workers and the market for its products). Some economists, e.g., Finis Welch (1981), have developed theories about the effects of affirmative action programs that ascribe initial group differences in wages and employment purely to supply, i.e., differences in skills acquired by workers in different groups. More common (especially in the empirical work reviewed here) are theories that result in lower demand for women or for minorities because of discrimination. Various reasons have been offered to explain differential demand: firm owners might indulge in a "taste" for discrimination by paying white workers more than black workers, for example. Alternatively, customers or employees might practice discrimination in such a way that productivity declines, in turn lowering the demand for women and people of color.

The basic effects of an enforced antidiscrimination program are easily predicted from the model: demand for women or for minorities will increase, resulting in higher wages and employment for that group.[6] In some policy models, changes in the wage and employment relative to the white or male group depend on other factors (e.g., Johnson and Welch 1976), but most of the empirical models predict greater wage and employment equality between groups as the result of policy.

Other effects of policy depend on the extent to which the model assumes differential productivity of workers. For instance, in developing a convenient model, Leonard (1984c) starts with a firm with a taste for discrimination but also implicitly assumes that white men are more productive. Thus his finding that affirmative action programs have increased the employment of black and female labor also implies some efficiency loss for the firm. Because he does not directly test this assumption (although he indirectly tests it in Leonard [1984a]), he draws no conclusions about efficiency loss.

When different parts of the economy face different requirements, the outcomes produced by policy become more complicated. This complication is particularly important in the interpretation of federal contractor requirement studies (discussed below), when federal contractors face stronger affirmative action requirements than noncontractors do. If female or minority workers can and do move from jobs with noncontractors to jobs in contractor firms because they expect less discrimination, then wages or employment may change *without* any direct changes in demand for those workers. In general, the papers reviewed in this report implicitly or explicitly assume that wages adjust to "clear" the labor market, i.e., everyone who wants a job at the going wage has one, and there are no unemployed people willing to work for a lower wage. But, if the wage does not adjust and if there are more workers than job openings, then the movement of workers from the applicant pool of noncontractors to the applicant pool of contractors may not affect the relative wages or employment of women or minorities.

Alternative Economic Models. Other kinds of economic models of labor markets drop the strict neoclassical analogy of workers to commodities. Institutional and radical models focus on the social nature of work and the role of power in the relationship between workers and managers. These models commonly revolve around the concept of an internal labor market in which firms create their own labor supply by training and promoting workers. While market forces (such as the changes in product market or in labor supply) might push wages and employment in one direction or another, many other social and political forces also influence wages and employment, preventing either a neat determination of a market wage that results in no unemployment or a clear prediction of the effects of antidiscrimination policy. The effects of policy will also depend on how it alters the norms and institutional structures that guide the behavior of firms and of white and male workers, as well as the interaction of firms and majority workers with minority and female workers.

Research on policy effectiveness drawn from these non-neoclassical models of the labor market have largely focused on case studies, which are not reviewed in this report. One exception, discussed below, is Paul Osterman's 1982 analysis of female quit rates within the context of an internal labor market. As a result of the selection process of both this report and of mainstream economists, the questions that might be asked by institutional or radical labor economists can only be partially answered. Through what channels does enforcement pressure influence firms' employment decisions? Within what kind of firm is pressure most effective? What effect do macroeconomic conditions have? What effect does a change in the funding of enforcement agencies or in the enforcement tools used have on employment outcomes? Is there evidence of competition among workers for jobs? Aggregated and highly quantitative data cannot answer many of these questions, but results from such studies should be consistent with evidence from other sources, i.e., case studies, and vice versa. The studies reviewed here offer evaluations of the usefulness of some of the most important enforcement tools, such as class-action lawsuits, compliance reviews, and goals and timetables.

TITLE VII ENFORCEMENT: EFFECTS ON EMPLOYEES, MEASURED OVER TIME

One way of estimating the effects of policy would be to compare the behavior of employers subject to Title VII requirements with that of employers not subject to them. But as was previously noted, using this method is difficult because of the widespread coverage of the law. As a result, studies of enforcement effects either compare labor market outcomes—mainly wages and employment—over time (those studies are reviewed below) or take advantage of geographic variations in enforcement through a cross-sectional examination (reviewed later). The study findings are summarized in Table 2.

The variables used to measure the enforcement of Title VII in these studies are less than ideal. Some of the variables are based on measures from the EEOC budget and are good indicators of federal effort and attention. However, other variables, such as the number or rate of complaints or lawsuits, reflect not only enforcement effort but the degree of discrimination as well. Because Title VII enforcement is complaint-driven (unlike enforcement of Executive Order 11246), complaint-related variables inevitably mix changes in the incidence of discrimination with changes in enforcement agency effort and re-sources. Variables based simply on the complaints filed therefore have the least value in identifying enforcement effort, while those based on settlements or investigations have much more value in this regard. That EEOC investigates a complaint should have more impact on employers than the mere filing of a complaint by one of their workers. In other words, if discrimination increases and EEOC investigations increase by the same amount, employers' future actions should be influenced by the investigations, giving the variable an enforcement interpretation.

An important related issue for these studies concerns the possibility that changes in the outcomes, such as relative levels of black employment or wages, might also be determined by the degree of discrimination. This would change the causal direction assumed by those using statistical models: instead of the number of complaints influencing the economic outcome (assumed when using multiple regression techniques), the unequal economic outcomes themselves may lead to more complaints. Careful researchers adjust for this possibility.

Richard Freeman (1973) began a continuing debate about the role of Title VII in the observed improvement from 1948 to 1972 in nonwhite workers' incomes relative to those of white workers.[7] Freeman measures antidiscrimination policy efforts as cumulative expenditures by the EEOC per nonwhite worker, a measure that he emphasizes is "an index of activity, not a measure of effectiveness." He uses multiple regression analysis, a common method for finding economic relationships in data, to separate out and quantify the factors thought to determine the variable to be explained (known as the "dependent variable").

In this 1973 study, Freeman attempts to explain why the relative income and occupational status of black workers have changed over time by estimating the effects of the business cycle, relative education, and the policy variable. After accounting for and removing the effects of other important factors, Freeman finds that EEOC activity has a positive and generally significant effect[8] on many measures of black workers' economic situation. For most of those measures, the EEOC effect was greater for black women than for black men. Freeman's findings suggest that EEOC enforcement increased the demand for black workers, resulting in the improvement in their economic position observed in the 1960s.

Richard Butler and James Heckman (1977) show that Freeman's result holds up even during the recession of the mid-1970s. They criticize Freeman's general conclusion that the demand for nonwhite workers had increased, however, arguing that relative incomes could have risen from a drop in the black labor supply, a drop they attribute to low-income black workers leaving the labor force in response to welfare programs whose benefits were more attractive than the wages they had been earning. Adding variables for relative labor force participation and estimating Freeman's model using a different statistical procedure[9] makes the EEOC effect disappear for both black men and black women. Using Freeman's original method, they also find that the EEOC variable affects outcomes for black workers only in the South.

In response to Butler and Heckman, Freeman (1981) uses their method with a slightly different policy measure[10] and corrected Butler-Heckman data. Freeman again finds a positive and significant effect of EEOC expenditures on nonwhite workers' income relative to that of white workers.

Without comment on the corrected data, Charles Brown (1982) notes that a falling black labor supply would have been unlikely to account for the observed trend, since the relative decline in labor force participation among both men and women would have been offset by the rising black share of the population. He also suggests that looking at aggregated data over time does not allow for a convincing statistical separation of the supply-and-demand effects.

This controversy over the effect of the withdrawal of low wage-earning black men from the labor force has since moved into the realm of more detailed individual-level studies. As reviewed in James Heckman (1989), these studies indicate that the effects of this withdrawal could account for some of the improvement in relative black male incomes in the 1960s and 1970s, but could not account for all of it.

TITLE VII ENFORCEMENT: EFFECTS ON EMPLOYEES, MEASURED BY LOCAL VARIATION

In an ambitious series of articles, Andrea Beller (1977, 1978, 1979, 1982) argues for a more complex understanding of the consequences of antidiscrimination policy, suggesting that Title VII could have conflicting effects on wages and employment of black workers. For instance, if firms are forced to pay black and white workers the same wage, the employers can still accommodate their desire to discriminate by simply hiring fewer black workers. If discrimination in hiring is forbidden, firms can simply pay black workers a lower wage.

But Title VII forbids both kinds of discrimination, eliminating a firm's usual adjustment mechanism and leading to either higher labor costs or unhappiness with the racial mix of the firm's workforce. Given imperfect enforcement, firms will weigh the costs of compliance against the costs of avoidance, which depend on possible penalties and the likelihood of being caught. Firms can also avoid the employment requirements through migration to predominantly white areas or changes in production techniques that could reduce relative black employment and wages. Emphasizing the enforcement of the equal wage requirement could therefore lead to declines in relative black employment, as firms adjust by shrinking in size or by substituting white workers. Thus the wage and employment provisions of Title VII could have perverse and conflicting results.

Effects on Black Wages and Employment. In an attempt to separate these effects with the imperfect data available, Beller (1978) focuses on differences between states in relative black male employment (for the economy as a whole and for firms filing EEO-1 reports) and wages from 1950 to 1970. Enforcement pressure is measured as the number of racial discrimination charges filed (separately categorized as either employment-related or wage-related) and accepted by the EEOC between 1968 and 1970, divided by a proxy for the number of workers in covered firms. Standard multiple regression analysis presumes that the various factors to be separated out determine the dependent variable, not the other way around. Because in this case the causal determination could easily go in the other direction, i.e., low levels of black male employment could lead to more discrimination complaints, Beller also uses a more sophisticated technique (two-stage least squares) to highlight the effect of enforcement pressure on wages and employment.

Beller finds that the total effect of Title VII on employment was positive for black officials, managers, and craftsmen and negative for professionals and office and clerical workers. To examine the effect of Title VII on wages, Beller uses census data on the percentage change in the ratio of nonwhite to white male wages (1959 to 1969) and income (1959 to 1969 and 1949 to 1959). The combined effect of the two provisions reduced black men's wages.

Curiously, the 1968 to 1970 complaint variables have a significant effect on relative incomes in the 1949 to 1959 equation, that is, *before* passage of the Civil Rights Act. Charges of employment discrimination are associated with lower relative black incomes and charges of wage discrimination with higher black incomes in the earlier period. This suggests that either complaints in the late 1960s are related to some influence present before the Act was passed or reverse causation is a legitimate concern requiring the more sophisticated statistical procedure. In sum, Beller finds support for the hypothesis that Title VII enforcement has conflicting effects for black men, affecting their wages negatively and their employment positively.

Other commentators (Brown 1982; Butler and Heckman 1977) have criticized Beller's choice of variables and use of state-level data. More important, her results regarding the separate effects of Title VII are very sensitive to the statistical technique used. Beller reports her "best" results, but as she herself points out, even these are not always statistically significant at standard levels, especially those using the most appropriate procedures. Overall, the evidence for conflicts between the effect of the wage and employment provisions of Title VII on black men must be regarded as weak.

Effects on the Male-Female Earnings Gap. Beller extends her work in three other papers that use similar data and methodologies.[11] In Beller (1979), she attempts to measure the effect of EEO laws on the male-female earnings gap. Again, she takes advantage of variations in the earnings gap by state, using the Current Population Survey for 1968, 1972, and 1975. One measure of Title VII enforcement is the ratio, in

1970, of completed EEOC investigations into sex discrimination charges to the number of women employed in the private or public sector in each state group. A second measure, the ratio of successful settlements to attempted settlements, is intended to capture the probability of paying a penalty if caught. Beller accounts for the effects of the federal contract compliance program with the ratio of federal purchases to net output in 50 industry groups.

Beller concludes that Title VII investigations tend to increase both male and female earnings, but successful settlements usually decrease them (although the significance varies somewhat over the two time periods investigated; two periods were chosen to try to pick up the effect of the 1972 amendments giving the EEOC the right to initiate lawsuits). The significance also varies over the public/private sector distinction. Beller suggests that the positive effect on men's earnings reflects an increase in firms' hiring of men when required to pay women more. In most cases, the enforcement effect tends to be stronger for women, reducing the earnings gap, but the difference in effects is not statistically distinguishable from zero. This means her conclusion, that Title VII reduced the wage gap by 7 percent overall (14 percent in the private sector), is overstated, and Title VII may have had no impact on the wage gap. (The federal purchases variable had no impact on the differential.) In a related paper (1977), Beller shows that both investigations and settlements had a net positive effect on changes in earnings for both white and black women over the same time period.

Effects on Women's Job Opportunity. In a later paper (1982), Beller seeks to determine whether EEO programs increased women's access to jobs usually held by men in 1967, 1971, and 1974. She investigates changes in the probability of a woman's holding a "male" occupation, defined as one where the share of male employment exceeds the share of men in the labor force by more than five percentage points. Applying the same enforcement variables as used in her 1979 study, Beller finds that enforcement does improve women's probability of being in a male occupation in the latest year, 1974.[12] Contract compliance improves the probability for women in all three years studied.

Beller finds that the combined effect of Title VII and the contract compliance program between 1967 and 1974 narrowed by 6.6 percent the difference between men's and women's probability of being employed in a male occupation. Although the policy effect is small and the estimated models do not explain occupational position very well, the effects of EEO programs are greater than the effects of changes in women's labor supply.

EEOC COMPLAINTS AND CLASS-ACTION SUITS: EFFECTS ON EMPLOYEES

Steven Shulman (1987), who also divides up racial discrimination complaints received by the EEOC into wage and employment complaints, examines the relationship between complaints and employment-to-population ratios across metropolitan areas in 1980. Shulman's policy variable is similar to one of Beller's, with the number of complaints in 1980 being divided by the size of the black labor force, although he does not interpret this as an enforcement measurement.[13] His hypothesis—that more employment discrimination complaints reflect more discrimination which, in turn, reduces employment for black workers—is corroborated by his statistical analysis, which shows a significant inverse correlation between complaints and employment-to-population ratios. Unfortunately, Shulman does not use the proper statistical technique to account for the issue raised by Beller, namely, that a low employment-to-population ratio for black workers could itself increase the number of complaints filed. This last possibility would reverse the causal link assumed in Shulman's analysis.

At first glance, Shulman's findings might seem to contradict other studies showing that greater enforcement activity leads to higher employment of black workers. Since complaints can reflect both the degree of discrimination in an area *and* the extent of enforcement, the construction and interpretation of the statistical analysis require some care. Beller's interpretation of the frequency of complaints as an enforcement measure is appropriate since she is comparing black employment before and after the complaints were filed. Shulman looks at the contemporaneous relationship of discrimination complaints to employment, making his interpretation of complaints as discrimination justifiable and his conclusion plausible—discrimination is likely to reduce black employment.[14] (Shulman's study is included in this review because of the apparent similarity with Beller's analysis, although Shulman's empirical project and interpretations differ from Beller's.)

Leonard (1984a), in contrast, argues that discrimination complaints are not a good measure of enforcement because of the time lag involved, the low probability of a negotiated settlement or a favorable court decision, and the lack of follow-up to monitor compliance. Instead, Leonard measures enforcement by the number of Title VII class action suits (decided between 1964 and 1981) per corporation in each industry in each state. In addition to the direct effects such litigation has, Leonard notes that it can also establish wide-ranging legal precedents that would have spillover effects on other industries or geographical areas.

He concludes that this litigation pressure did increase black workers' proportion of the labor force in EEO-1-reporting establishments between 1966 and 1978. This positive effect, which is separate from the effect of federal contract compliance pressure, is particularly strong in white-collar occupations. Leonard also reports that the effects for white women are sometimes negative but usually statistically insignificant.

Summary of Title VII Studies. All of these measures of Title VII enforcement pressure are indirect and imperfect, especially as firms adapt institutionally to EEO requirements—a complaint that may have once provoked a crisis response may later be dealt with bureaucratically and systematically. Ideally, we would want to measure the effects of complaints and litigation on firms more directly, but the necessary data do not exist. Even if they did, it would be difficult to measure the impact of legal precedents, such as *Griggs* v. *Duke Power,*[15] that might alter firms' behavior even when firms are not subjected to direct enforcement pressure. Given the imperfection of the measures, however, the fact that these variables are usually found to be systematically related to the wages and employment of black workers (and, to a lesser extent, of white women) is somewhat remarkable and difficult to dismiss even though the benefits of EEO policy at historical levels of enforcement are clearly small.

FEDERAL CONTRACT COMPLIANCE: EFFECTS OF EEO REQUIREMENTS

In contrast to the studies of Title VII effectiveness, research into the effects of the federal contract compliance programs has been able to measure pressure on firms more directly. The EEO-1 forms required of firms with more than 100 employees have been a rich data source for assessing the effect of the affirmative action requirement. Since all firms filing EEO-1 forms are covered by Title VII, differences in minority and female employment between contractor firms and noncontractor firms that are otherwise similar should reflect only the effect of the affirmative action plan. If noncontractor firms voluntarily or by court order adopt such plans, however, their minority and female employment levels may be higher, in which case the *estimated* contractor effect would be lower than the *actual* effect of affirmative action programs. None of the studies below make direct allowances for this possibility, probably as a result of data limitations.

As discussed earlier (see "Economic Theories of Discrimination"), according to neoclassical economic theory, changes in black or female employment can be the result of either changes in the firm's demand for their labor or changes in the number of black or female workers offering to work for the firm. Sorting out which forces are at work requires data on both wages and employment. If demand increases, then both wages and employment will increase because firms are competing to attract new employees. If supply increases, workers are more plentiful and must offer to work for a lower wage to attract a job offer, so wages fall and employment increases.

Unfortunately, the EEO-1 forms ask employers only to identify race, gender, and occupation, so the effect of affirmative action on wages must be measured indirectly. This has generally been approached in two ways: (1) by investigating changes in the relative occupational status of people of color or of white women within a firm, as measured by the average wage or income of people in each occupation, and (2) by using national data on individuals and matching some measure of federal pressure on contractors. The major studies have used similar strategies and models for investigating the effects of employment and occupational position on affirmative action (described in more technical detail in the Appendix).

Effects on Employment. Table 3 and Appendix Table A2 present the relative employment effects found in the studies, which cover the time period from 1966 to 1980. The effects of contractor status and of OFCCP compliance review are seen in the annual percentage change in the ratio of protected-group employment to white male employment. In most cases, the effects are not large. For instance, Orley Ashenfelter and James Heckman (1976) find that, on average, contractors increase the employment of black men relative to white men by 0.83 percent per year in the short run. The form of the variables is also clearly important; Jonathan Leonard finds larger effects in his 1984c study than in his 1984b study, using the same data but slightly different measures of firm growth and size.

No systematic pattern is clear over time, perhaps because of those differences in form and method. The most consistent employment benefits of affirmative action are for black men. Ashenfelter and Heckman (1976) find positive effects of affirmative action among federal contractors in the earliest study, but Morris Goldstein and Robert S. Smith (1976) do not find any in the next period and even find negative effects on white women. Goldstein and Smith's only other statistically significant effect is the positive impact compliance reviews have on black male employment. Leonard finds that black women and "other" men (mostly Asian and Latino) benefit the most in one study (1984b) while black men and women fare best according to the other study (1984c). A study not included in Table 2, by James Heckman and Kenneth Wolpin (1976), finds positive contractor effects in Chicago over the 1970-to-1973 period for the employment of black men and other minorities but negative effects for women (although statistically insignificant) and for white men. In an unpublished study of national data from 1980 to 1984, Leonard (1990) finds negative effects: "... both male and female black employment grew more slowly among contractors than noncontractors" (p. 58).

It is not clear why the findings differ. Aside from the differences noted above, different time periods could clearly be a reason. As noted earlier, the quantity and quality of OFCCP enforcement have varied over the years. If OFCCP enforcement is responsible for reducing discrimination and increasing employers' demand for people of color and for white women, generating the positive contractor effects measured, then variations either in enforcement or in firms' desire to discriminate might be responsible for variations in the contractor effect. Leonard, for instance, suggests a rough correlation with enforcement intensity. Enforcement effort was low during the earliest and most recent periods studied, resulting in small or negative effects, and it was relatively strong in the 1974-to-1980 period when the largest measured impacts occur.

Goldstein and Smith (1976) suggest that different macroeconomic conditions could account for at least some of the differences between the studies' findings, while Brown argues that higher unemployment should not be related to OFCCP enforcement efforts. While Brown may be correct, in a world of imperfect enforcement macroeconomic conditions might overwhelm other considerations in firms' compliance decisions and could result in layoffs that reverse firms' previous affirmative action efforts.

Although the studies generally find that having a federal contract is related to relatively higher levels of black employment, if not of white female employment, some researchers doubt that this association necessarily reflects an increased demand caused by the affirmative action requirement. As many economists have pointed out (e.g., Brown 1982; or Donohue and Heckman 1991), relative increases in black employment levels in the contractor sector could be the result of the voluntary movement of workers between contractor employment and noncontractor employment. Further investigations into this possibility will likely be limited by the quality of available data, however.

Effects on Occupational Status. The lack of matching wage data is one important obstruction to the future of affirmative action research. If both wages and employment were observed to rise, it would make a strong case that affirmative action leads firms to increase demand for protected workers. An alternative way to measure wage changes stemming from the contractor requirement is to use changes in occupational status as a proxy. The contract compliance program studies typically either (1) construct some index of occupational status by weighting employment in occupations by the median or mean earnings of the occupation, as found in CPS or census data, or (2) look at changes in employment within the different occupational categories defined by the EEO-1 reporting firms.

Those studies using the first approach apply a statistical method similar to that used for studying relative employment changes. Ashenfelter and Heckman (1976) find a small (and statistically insignificant) positive effect on occupational status of working for a contractor; Goldstein and Smith (1976) find a negative effect for white women and an insignificant positive effect for black women and black men; Leonard (1984b) finds that both contractor status and compliance reviews raise occupational status for *all* race-gender groups.

Studies taking the second approach reveal some other patterns of interest. Ashenfelter and Heckman's study shows that the largest significant positive effect on black men's employment was in the operatives category, while their employment actually declined in service, managerial, and professional categories. Heckman and Wolpin (1976) use just two categories, blue-collar and white-collar, and find that only in blue-collar occupations was there a higher proportion of black males in contractor firms, although even this effect was not statistically significant. In the blue-collar occupations, they find significantly higher employment in contractor establishments only for "other" men who, along with white men, also had significantly higher white-collar employment in contractor establishments. The effect of working for a contractor was negative and significant among blue-collar workers for white men and black women, and among white-collar workers for white women and black men and women.

These two studies led to the early conclusion that affirmative action mainly improves employment opportunities in the less-skilled occupations. For the 1974-to-1980 period, Leonard (1984b) uses more detailed categories and finds positive contractor and review effects on black men, black women, white women, and "other" men in many of the highest occupational categories, most consistently for managerial and professional jobs. As he suggests, perhaps his more positive results for this period are due to heightened enforcement.

Effects on Wages. In another study, Leonard (1986) attempts to estimate the effects of the affirmative action requirement on wages more directly. He measures policy pressure as the proportion of employment in an individual's metropolitan area and industry that is in federal contractor establishments. Leonard estimates the policy effect separately for 1973 and 1978 with CPS data and finds that the policy variable has a positive effect on both white *and* nonwhite men in both years, with a relatively larger impact on nonwhite men. He interprets this finding as evidence that the employment effects of the federal contract compliance program were caused by rising demand for black and other minority men rather than as evidence that these workers shifted from noncontractor into contractor firms.

Leonard also tests a second affirmative action "bifurcation" hypothesis, that of Welch (1981), who suggests that low-skilled black workers have been hurt by affirmative action. Contrary to this hypothesis, Leonard finds an even larger contractor effect on wages for nonwhite men with little education. Leonard's 1984b study also refutes the bifurcation hypothesis by showing that employment in low-skilled occupations usually benefits from the total impact of both contractor status and compliance reviews.

Effects on Quit Rates. Osterman (1982) presents evidence that the contract compliance program's effects extend beyond hiring to improvements in opportunities within firms. He finds that the probability of quitting a job for a nationally representative sample of women was lower for women in industries with high levels of enforcement.[16] Osterman measures two different enforcement variables over the 1977-to-1979 period: (1) the share of federal government purchases in the industry and (2) that share times total OFCCP compliance reviews in the industry divided by industry employment. Using either measure, Osterman's results show that policy pressure significantly reduces the rate at which female workers quit their jobs, with stronger effects found among women age 30 and under.

FEDERAL CONTRACT COMPLIANCE EFFECTS: EXAMINING THE CAUSAL MECHANISMS AT WORK

Job Reclassification. Several other issues have been raised throughout this literature that deserve comment. Smith and Welch (1984) compared occupational data from the CPS with data from EEO-1 forms and found discrepancies in the patterns of change in the race and gender composition of the same occupational categories over the 1966-to-1980 period. They interpret this as evidence that firms have responded to federal pressure by reclassifying the occupations of people of color and white women rather than actually hiring more into certain occupational categories. Smith and Welch's finding seems less insidious when one notes that the discrepancies they point out in the managerial and professional categories balance each other out: the shifts seem to be mainly *within* two high-skilled categories rather than from below.

Selection of Firms for Contracts. A second issue concerning the accuracy of the apparent positive effect of contractor status is what economists call "selection bias." Heckman and Wolpin (1976) question whether the observed difference in relative black employment in contractor firms results from the contractor selection process. If firms are rewarded with federal contracts for having high levels of protected-group employment, then observing higher levels of minority and female employment among contractors does not necessarily reflect affirmative action pressure.

In their investigation of this possibility, Heckman and Wolpin find that employing higher proportions of black men does improve a firm's probability of getting a contract, but the effect is statistically insignificant. Leonard (1984c) presents results with a much stronger conclusion refuting this potential bias: the probability of being a contractor rises as the proportion of white men in an establishment rises, but falls as the level and percentage of women or people of color rises. Thus higher relative employment of black workers in contractor establishments is not simply the result of the government awarding contracts to the "better" firms to begin with.

Selection of Contractors for Review. Further questions about the regulatory mechanisms at work have been raised by Charles Brown (1982). Leonard (1985a) finds a systematic process at work in reviews. Rather than targeting establishments that are likely to be practicing discrimination, such as establishments with all white male employees, the OFCCP seems to target large establishments with higher proportions of professional and managerial workers. Leonard infers that this represents a policy goal of redistributing income: as enforcement leads to a wider distribution of the higher paying jobs, the incomes of formerly excluded groups will rise.

Leonard's work represents the most thorough examination of the tools of OFCCP pressure. Using data from compliance reviews conducted at establishments that had been reviewed more than once, Leonard (1985c) analyzes the effect of various measures of pressure on firms, e.g., hours expended by review officers and progress reports required. None of the measures has a consistent effect on the employment of different groups.

Goal Setting. Leonard finds that employment goals set by firms during the reviews to correct underutilization provide the best predictions about future race-gender proportions in the workforce even though firms consistently overestimate how many people in *all* groups they will hire. Also, firms do not seem to view these goals as quotas: Leonard (1985c) finds that "goals are not being fulfilled with the rigidity one would expect of quotas."[17] Black women constitute the one exception to this conclusion—their employment grows faster than predicted by the goals.

Overall, then, compliance reviews themselves must have some shock effect on firms since other components of regulatory pressure are not found to have any systematic effect on later employment outcomes. Further, firms take their goals seriously but not as rigid quotas.

Growing Versus Shrinking Contractors. Studies comparing contractors with noncontractors reveal other factors influencing the employment of black workers, factors that are important in understanding the influence of policy. One finding concerns the differential effect of policy on growing versus shrinking contractor firms. Both Heckman and Wolpin (1976) and Leonard (1984c) find that growing contractors have higher proportions of employment of certain groups. The Heckman and Wolpin finding is stronger for white men, however, so growth results in no relative improvement for black workers.

Nevertheless, Leonard shows that not only do black men, black women, white women, and "other" men benefit more than white men from growth regardless of contractor status, but the contractor effect is significantly higher in growing establishments. This suggests that affirmative action has not meant displacement of white male workers but an increasing share of *new* jobs for people of color and white women.

Regional Effects. Another important finding from some of these studies is the improvement in the status of black workers in the South, regardless of contractor status (Ashenfelter and Heckman 1976; Leonard 1984c; Goldstein and Smith 1976). James Heckman and Brook Payner (1989) look more closely at federal policy in the South. They analyze employment and wage data for South Carolina to argue for what Heckman and Donohue (1991) call a "more refined view of federal policy." Although the enforcement mechanism that Heckman and Payner point to was the EEOC's targeting of the Southern textile industry in 1966 and 1967, their most direct measure of federal pressure is the value of defense contracts per county. This policy variable does have a positive and significant effect on the level of black employment (at the county level), but it does not have as large an effect on black status as an as-yet unexplained post-1964 trend.

EFFECTS ON FIRM PERFORMANCE

As discussed above ("Economic Theories of Discrimination"), discrimination theorists have hypothesized that EEO policies that force firms to change their hiring practices could lead to reduced worker productivity, and therefore, lower firm profits. Evidence presented in the preceding sections of this paper suggests that firms' behavior did change in response to EEO policies, but far less evidence exists on the effect of those employment changes on profitability.

Leonard (1984a) uses a highly aggregated approach to measure changes in the industry-level productivities of women and nonwhite men relative to white men for manufacturing industries in 1966 and 1977. He admits that his estimates of productivity are somewhat imprecise, but he does find increases in relative productivity of women and nonwhite men that cannot be completely attributed to their entry into more highly skilled occupations or to relative increases in education. He concludes that firms are not hiring less qualified black or female workers as a result of affirmative action pressure, as the reverse discrimination hypothesis holds.

Joni Hersch (1991) measures the impact of announcements of EEO lawsuits, decisions, and settlements in the *Wall Street Journal* on the subject firm's stock price. She finds negative impacts of announcements on stock prices only in the short run, mainly the two days before and after the announcement. Over longer periods, Hersch does not find abnormal negative returns for those firms. Class action suits have a larger, somewhat longer effect, but even that disappears after 30 days. She suggests that investors respond to this news because of expectations of legal expenses, penalties, and possible increases in labor costs if firms must change their practices. She concludes that, over the longer run, the impact of announcements disappears because it is relatively unimportant compared to the other forces influencing a firm's equity value.

QUESTIONS FOR FURTHER RESEARCH

After almost 20 years of careful study, questions and concerns remain. The pattern of gains is difficult to explain: black women and "other" men apparently gain the most from the contractor program, followed by black men, who show slightly smaller gains, and white women, who get a mixed effect from the program. Why does the contractor compliance program seem to have such a weak effect on white women's employment gains? The massive general increase in women's employment—in contractors *and* noncontractors—only answers part of that question.

Even more troubling, the general pattern of gains from affirmative action and equal employment opportunity enforcement is difficult to square with other measures of labor market position, especially unemployment rates. The largest gains measured in any of these studies occurred in the second half of the 1970s, a period of rising relative unemployment rates for black males and females and falling relative rates for white females (Badgett 1990). None of the contractor studies explicitly accounts for the effects of unemployment on the operation of labor markets and discrimination, either on firms' behavior or on differences between contractors and noncontractors.[18] The importance of this omission is evident if, for example, high unemployment makes the firm less likely to hire or more likely to lay off women or minority workers because of seniority systems or because of white or male workers' pressure on the firm. In that case, the failure to include unemployment in the empirical analysis means that any change in employment attributed to having a federal contract may be in fact a result of the unemployment situation. If we see little or no difference in the change in employment between contractors and noncontractors, this finding could result from the different cyclical sensitivities of contractors versus noncontractors. The Title VII studies do take into account differences in unemployment rates among the local labor markets studied, but only Shulman's (1987) study attempts to *explain* the enormous difference between black and white unemployment rates. The resolution of this apparent contradiction between progress at one level and deterioration at another—between gains in black employment resulting from affirmative action and EEOC policies on the one hand and the overall worsening of black unemployment on the other—awaits future researchers.

The other major weakness of the studies reviewed in this report concerns the actual mechanisms and institutions through which this policy pressure works. Studies using more detailed measures of particular enforcement instruments provide little insight into highly successful or efficient enforcement methods or into the institutional processes through which they work. We know little from these studies about how long it takes firms to react to changes in enforcement pressure from various directions (courts, agencies, etc.) and about how adaptation to such pressure is balanced against other market pressures.

Overall, these studies tell us that policy can improve the employment and wages of people of color and white women, but the effects so far have been small. This may mean that either historical levels of enforcement have been inadequate or that other more powerful political and economic forces have counteracted the influence of policy.

NOTES

1. Later legislation extended the policy of forbidding employers to discriminate on the basis of some other characteristics unrelated to job performance, e.g., to age and disability. This report will not take up these issues.

2. The Supreme Court has indicated that EEOC testing guidelines were entitled to "great deference" in *Griggs* v. *Duke Power Co.* The meaning of "deference" with respect to the more recent Uniform Guidelines on Employee Selection Procedures has been subject to different interpretations (Schlei and Grossman 1983, 96).

3. U.S. House of Representatives, Committee on Education and Labor, 1987.

4. For two different perspectives, see Cain (1986) and Reich (1981).

5. The neoclassical model also suggests that as long as wages can adjust in response to the two conflicting forces, unemployment should not exist. In the real world, of course, there are many barriers to the free movement of wages and workers, but one of the values of this theoretical approach is that the anticipated effects of such barriers, including discrimination, can be clearly identified.

6. More precisely, the demand curve for female or minority workers will shift out.

7. Until 1972, the racial categories in published data were "white" and "nonwhite." The vast majority in the "nonwhite" category were black workers.

8. As used in this paper, "statistical significance" means that the probability is very low (usually 5 percent or less) that the observed effect resulted simply by chance and therefore that no *true* effect exists in the population being studied. An "insignificant" effect is one that, although it might seem large, cannot be considered to be different from zero, since another study using a different sample is likely to result in a very different measured effect.

9. This technique, two-stage least squares, assumes a more complicated relationship between the variables than in a simple multiple regression.

10. The log of cumulative EEOC expenditures per nonwhite worker.

11. When possible, in all four papers Beller also takes into account other factors influencing wages and employment such as education and region.

12. Curiously, enforcement also improves men's probability of being in a male occupation, according to Beller; for both women and men to show increases

in the proportion working in such occupations, they must have been growing relative to the labor force as a whole.

13. Shulman does not mention the EEOC response to these complaints, i.e. whether the EEOC accepted or investigated these complaints.

14. Although this conclusion may seem obvious, it is also possible that discrimination reduces only wages or occupational status and *not* employment.

15. The U.S. Supreme Court's 1971 decision in *Griggs* v. *Duke Power* (401 U.S. 424) caused many employers to reexamine the mechanisms they were using to assess hiring eligibility, job performance, and promotions. *Griggs* set a new standard of compliance with Title VII of the Civil Rights Act. It ruled that employers could not use instruments (such as employment tests) that had a "disparate impact" on protected groups, even if the instruments appeared neutral on their face, unless they could be shown to "have a demonstrable relationship to performance on the job."

As Welch (1981, 128) notes: "This places the burden of proof on employers for requirements like a high school degree or acceptable exam scores to demonstrate that those not satisfying the requirements are unable to perform adequately."

16. Osterman's data are from the University of Michigan's Panel Survey of Income Dynamics.

17. Leonard (1985c, 18).

18. Leonard (1984c) shows that contractors are more likely to be found in the cyclically sensitive manufacturing industries, for instance.

Table 1
Surveys of Economic Literature Related to Affirmative Action

Butler & Heckman (1977)

Conclusion: Affirmative action policy has ambiguous or negative effects on black workers' wages and employment.

Comment: In own calculations, uses incorrect data.

Brown (1982)

Conclusion: Time-series studies show that affirmative action policy contributes to improvement in blacks' labor market position. Some studies show that federal-contractor status has a positive effect for black men, but these studies are vulnerable to criticism.

Leonard (1989)

Conclusion: Affirmative action policy has a negligible effect on white women's employment, possibly because of an increase in the supply of white female workers. Policy is more helpful for black women, though they gain no more from it than black men.

Leonard (1990)

Conclusion: Federal contract compliance and Title VII have a positive impact on minorities.

Donohue & Heckman (1991)

Conclusion: Federal civil rights enforcement (housing, education, and employment) in the South in the 1960s led to an improvement in blacks' overall economic status.

Comment: Focus is on men.

TABLE 2
SUMMARY OF STUDIES ON THE EFFECTS OF TITLE VII

Freeman (1973)

Period: 1946-72

Policy Variable: Cumulated real EEOC expenditures per nonwhite worker.

Conclusion: Enforcement of Title VII leads to increases in black incomes relative to incomes of white workers (after separating out the effects of business cycles).

Butler & Heckman (1977)

Period: 1948-74

Policy Variable: Same as for Freeman 1973.

Conclusion: The effect of Title VII enforcement (measured as expenditures) on labor force participation is negligible once the effect of other government programs is considered.

Comment: Uses incorrect data.

Beller (1977)

Period: 1967-74

Policy Variables: (1) The number of completed EEOC investigations in 1974, divided by the number of women in the labor force, per state, by private or public sector.
                   (2) The ratio of settlements to attempted settlements.

Conclusion: The enforcement of Title VII, as measured by both policy variables, has a positive impact on the earnings of white and black women.

Beller (1978)

Period: 1966-70 and 1950-70

Policy Variable: The number of racial discrimination charges filed and accepted by EEOC, divided by the number of workers in covered firms, by state.

Conclusion: The wage and employment provisions of Title VII may have contradictory effects; if wages are equalized, discrimination may appear in employment, and vice versa.

Comment: Studies men only; many findings are not statistically significant.

Beller (1979)

Period: 1967-74

Policy Variables: Same as for Beller 1977.

Conclusion: The enforcement of Title VII increases the demand for women workers and

Continued

—

Table 2 Continued

reduces the male-female earnings gap by 7 percent overall (and by 14 percent in the private sector).

Freeman (1981)

Period:	1948-75
Policy Variable:	(Log of the variable used in Freeman 1973) + 1.
Conclusion:	Title VII has a positive effect on the ratio of nonwhite to white earnings (using the same method as Butler and Heckman [1977] but with corrected data).

Beller (1982)

Period:	1967-74
Policy Variables:	Same as for Beller 1977.
Conclusion:	The enforcement of Title VII increases women's likelihood of entering male occupations.

Leonard (1984a)

Period:	1966-78
Policy Variable:	The number of Title VII class-action lawsuits (decided between 1964 and 1981) per corporation, by industry and by state.
Conclusion:	Title VII class-action litigation has a positive impact on black workers' employment rate.

Shulman (1987)

Period:	1980
Policy Variable:	The number of EEOC wage and employment discrimination complaints, divided by the size of the black labor force.
Conclusion:	Higher levels of EEOC discrimination complaints lead to lower employment-to-population ratios in metropolitan areas.
Comment:	Measurements contained erroneous effects (not policy effects) of changes.

TABLE 3
SUMMARY OF STUDIES ON THE EFFECTS OF THE FEDERAL CONTRACT COMPLIANCE PROGRAM

Ashenfelter & Heckman (1976)

Period: 1966-70

Conclusion: Federal-contractor status has a positive effect on the relative employment of black men and a positive, though insignificant, effect on their occupational status.

Comment: Only studied men; in part of paper, only studied firms with at least one black and one white worker.

Goldstein & Smith (1976)

Period: 1970-72

Conclusion: Federal-contractor status has a significant negative effect on white women and an insignificant negative effect on black men's and women's employment; compliance reviews have a positive effect on black men, so the overall effect of the contract compliance program is positive for black men's employment.

Heckman & Wolpin (1976)

Period: 1970-73

Conclusion: Federal-contractor status has a positive effect on black men's and "Other" men's employment rates but a negative effect on white women, black women, and white men. The positive effects are limited to blue-collar workers.

Comment: Chicago data only.

Osterman (1982)

Period: 1977-79

Conclusion: Two measures of compliance pressure lower the probability of women's quitting their jobs, suggesting greater opportunities within firms.

Leonard (1984b)

Period: 1974-80

Conclusion: Federal-contractor status and reviews have a significant positive effect on the employment of black men, black women, white women, and "Other" men, not only among blue-collar workers but in higher occupational categories as well. Contractor status also has a significant positive effect on occupational status for all groups.

Continued

—

Table 3 Continued

Leonard (1984c)

Period: 1974-80

Conclusion: Federal-contractor status has a significant positive effect on the employment of black men, black women, white women, and "Other" men.

Comment: Uses different variables from Leonard 1984b.

Leonard (1985a)

Period: 1975-79

Conclusion: The OFCCP is more likely to review establishments with higher proportions of nonclerical white-collar workers, suggesting it pursues a policy goal of redistribution of income.

Leonard (1985c)

Period: Late 1970s

Conclusion: Goals set by firms during OFCCP reviews are good predictors of those firms' future workforces even though they are not fulfilled rigidly.

Comment: Sample was of closely monitored contractors.

Leonard (1986)

Period: 1973 & 1978

Conclusion: Using the proportion of SMSA and industry employment in federal contractor firms as a measure of affirmative action pressure, Leonard finds that the greater the affirmative action pressure the larger the wage increases, for both white and nonwhite men. Wage effects were larger for nonwhite men than for white men, and among nonwhite men larger for those who were less educated. Leonard concludes that wages rose because demand for nonwhite men increased overall as a result of affirmative action requirements.

Heckman & Payner (1989)

Period: 1947-71

Conclusion: The value of defense contracts per county in South Carolina in the 1960s had a significant positive impact on the counties' black male employment.

TABLE 4
SUMMARY OF STUDIES ON AFFIRMATIVE ACTION'S EFFECTS ON FIRM PERFORMANCE

Leonard (1984a)

Period: 1966 & 1977

Conclusion: Affirmative action increases the productivity of women and nonwhite men, suggesting that it is not causing firms to hire less qualified black or female workers.

Comment: Leonard notes that productivity is not measured precisely.

Hersch (1991)

Conclusion: The announcement of EEO lawsuits has a negative impact on the stock prices of firms being sued, but only in the short run; the effect disappears over time.

REFERENCES

Ashenfelter, Orley, and James Heckman. 1976. "Measuring the Effect of an Antidiscrimination Program." In *Evaluating the Labor Market Effects of Social Programs* (Research paper No. 120), edited by Orley Ashenfelter and James Blum. Princeton University, Department of Economics, Research Department, Industrial Relations Section.

Badgett, M. V. Lee. 1990. "Racial Differences in Unemployment Rates and Employment Opportunities." Ph.D. dissertation, University of California at Berkeley.

Becker, Gary S. 1957. *The Economics of Discrimination.* Chicago: University of Chicago Press.

Beller, Andrea H. 1977. "EEO Laws and the Earnings of Women." *Proceedings of the 29th Annual Winter Meeting.* Madison, Wis.: Industrial Relations Research Association.

——————. 1978. "The Economics of Enforcement of an Antidiscrimination Law: Title VII of the Civil Rights Act of 1964." *Journal of Law and Economics,* Vol. 21, No. 2.

——————. 1979. "The Impact of Equal Employment Opportunity Laws on the Male-Female Earnings Differential." In *Women in the Labor Market,* edited by Cynthia B. Lloyd, Emily S. Andrews, and Curtis L. Gilroy. New York: Columbia University Press.

——————. 1982. "Occupational Segregation by Sex: Determinants and Changes." *Journal of Human Resources,* Vol. 17, No. 3.

Brown, Charles. 1982. "The Federal Attack on Labor Market Discrimination: The Mouse that Roared?" In *Research in Labor Economics,* Vol. 5. Greenwich, Conn.: JAI Press.

Burbridge, Lynn. 1986. "Changes in Equal Employment Enforcement: What Enforcement Tells Us." *Review of Black Political Economics,* Vol. 15, No. 1.

Butler, Richard, and James J. Heckman. 1977. "The Government's Impact on the Labor Market Status of Black Americans: A Critical Review." In *Equal Rights and Industrial Relations,* edited by Farrell E. Bloch, et al. Madison, Wis.: Industrial Relations Research Association.

Cain, Glen G. 1986. "The Economic Analysis of Labor Market Discrimination: A Survey." In *Handbook of Labor Economics,* edited by Orley Ashenfelter and Richard Layard. Amsterdam: Elsevier Science Publishers.

Donohue, John H., and James Heckman. 1991. "Continuous Versus Episodic Change: The Impact of Civil Rights Policy on the Economic Status of Blacks." *Journal of Economic Literature,* Vol. 29, No. 4.

DuRivage, Virginia. 1985. "The OFCCP Under the Reagan Administration: Affirmative Action in Retreat." *Labor Law Journal,* Vol. 36, No. 6.

Freeman, Richard B. 1973. "Changes in the Labor Market for Black Americans, 1948-72." *Brookings Papers on Economic Activity,* No. 1.

———. 1981. "Black Economic Progress after 1964: Who Has Gained and Why?" In *Studies in Labor Markets,* edited by Sherwin Rosen. Chicago: University of Chicago Press.

Goldstein, Morris, and Robert S. Smith. 1976. "The Estimated Impact of the Antidiscrimination Program Aimed at Federal Contractors." *Industrial and Labor Relations Review,* Vol. 29, No. 4.

Heckman, James. 1989. "The Impact of Government on the Economic Status of Black Americans." In *The Question of Discrimination,* edited by Steven Shulman and William Darity, Jr. Middletown, Conn.: Wesleyan University Press.

Heckman, James, and Brook S. Payner. 1989. "Determining the Impact of Federal Antidiscrimination Policy on the Economic Status of Blacks: A Study of South Carolina." *American Economic Review,* Vol. 79, No. 1.

Heckman, James, and Kenneth Wolpin. 1976. "Does the Contract Compliance Program Work? An Analysis of Chicago Data." *Industrial and Labor Relations Review,* Vol. 29, July.

Hersch, Joni. 1991. "EEO Law and Firm Profitability." *Journal of Human Resources,* Vol. 26, No. 1.

Johnson, George E. and Finis Welch. 1976. "The Labor Market Implications of an Economywide Affirmative Action Program." *Industrial and Labor Relations Review,* Vol. 29, No. 4.

Leonard, Jonathan S. 1984a. "Anti-Discrimination or Reverse Discrimination: The Impact of Changing Demographics, Title VII and Affirmative Action on Productivity." *Journal of Human Resources,* Vol. 19, No. 2.

——————. 1984b. "Employment and Occupational Advance Under Affirmative Action." *Review of Economics and Statistics.* Vol. 66, No. 3.

——————. 1984c. "The Impact of Affirmative Action on Employment." *Journal of Labor Economics,* Vol. 2, No. 4.

——————. 1985a. "Affirmative Action as Earnings Redistribution: The Targeting of Compliance Reviews." *Journal of Labor Economics,* Vol. 3, No. 3.

——————. 1985b. "The Effect of Unions on the Employment of Blacks, Hispanics, and Women." *Industrial and Labor Relations Review,* Vol. 39, No. 1.

——————. 1985c. "What Promises are Worth: The Impact of Affirmative Action Goals." *Journal of Human Resources,* Vol. 20, No. 1.

——————. 1986. "Splitting Blacks? Affirmative Action and Earnings Inequality Within and Across Races." In *Proceedings of the 39th Annual Meeting.* Madison, Wis.: Industrial Relations Research Association.

——————. 1989. "Women and Affirmative Action." *Journal of Economic Perspectives,* Vol. 3, No. 1.

——————. 1990. "The Impact of Affirmative Action Regulation and Equal Employment Law on Black Employment." *Journal of Economic Perspectives,* Vol. 4, No. 4.

Osterman, Paul. 1982. "Affirmative Action and Opportunity: A Study of Female Quit Rates." *Review of Economics and Statistics,* Vol. 64, No. 4.

Reich, Michael. 1981. *Racial Inequality.* Princeton: Princeton University Press.

Schlei, Barbara L. and Paul Grossman. 1983. *Employment Discrimination Law,* 2nd edition. Washington, D.C.: Bureau of National Affairs.

Shulman, Steven. 1987. "Discrimination, Human Capital, and Black-White Unemployment: Evidence from Cities." *Journal of Human Resources,* Vol. 22, No. 3.

Smith, James P., and Finis Welch. 1984. "Affirmative Action and Labor Markets." *Journal of Labor Economics,* Vol. 2, No. 2.

U.S. Government Accounting Office. 1989. "Equal Employment Opportunities: EEOC and State Agencies Did Not Fully Investigate Discrimination Charges." Publication No. GAO/HRD-89-11. Washington, D.C.

U.S. House of Representatives, Committee on Education and Labor. 1987. "A Report on the Investigation of the Civil Rights Enforcement Activities of the Office of Federal Contract Compliance Programs, U.S. Department of Labor." Majority staff report (October). Washington, D.C.

Welch, Finis. 1986. "Affirmative Action and Its Enforcement." *American Economic Review,* Vol. 71, No. 2.

TABLE A1

SPECIFICATION OF EQUATIONS IN AFFIRMATIVE ACTION STUDIES

	ASHENFELTER & HECKMAN		GOLDSTEIN & SMITH		HECKMAN & WOLPIN	LEONARD (1984b)		LEONARD (1984c)	
Number of Establishments	24,535		74,563		3,677 (Chicago)	—68,690 (employment); 13,936 (occupational)—			
Estimating Method	Partial Adjustment				Adjustment for serial correlation	Weighted LS		Weighted LS	
Period Studied	1966–70		1970–72		1970–73	1974–80		1974–80	
VARIABLES	employment	occupational	employment	occupational	employment	employment	occupational	occupational	employment
Contractor Status (Year Measured)	X	X —(1970)—	X	X —(1970)—	X —(1973)—	X	X —(1974)—	X	X —(1974)—
Review		X	X	X	X	X			
Region		X	X	X	X	X	X		
Industry		X	X	X	X				
SMSA		X	X	X	X				
Lagged Dependent Variable		X	X						
Employment Shares of Other Groups		X	X						
Establishment Size (log)		X	X	X	X	X	X (log)		X
Growth in Employment		X	X	X	X				
Growth Rate		X			X				
White Collar		X	X						
In Multi-establishment Firms		X	X						

Note: These represent the main specifications discussed in each paper. Actual definitions of variables differ among papers.

TABLE A2
RELATIVE ANNUAL EMPLOYMENT EFFECTS ON AFFIRMATIVE ACTION

| | ASHENFELTER & HECKMAN | GOLDSTEIN & SMITH | | LEONARD (1984c) | | LEONARD (1984b) | |
	federal contractors	federal contractors	reviewed firms	federal contractors	reviewed firms	federal contractors	reviewed firms
Period Studied	*1966–70*	*1970–72*	*1970–72*	*1974–80*	*1974–80*	*1974–80*	*1974–80*
Black Women	NA	-0.3	0.4	2.2*	1.0*	0.8*	0.8*
Black Men	0.8* SR 12.9 LR	-0.1	0.8*	0.8*	1.3*	0.8*	0.8*
White Women	NA	-2.1*	-0.8*	0.7*	-0.5*	0.3*	-0.1*
Other Men	NA	NA	NA	1.5*	2.5*	0.3	1.2*

* Asterisk indicates significance at 5% level.

Note: Numbers in table represent percentage change in group employment relative to that of white men in firms that are federal contractors or have been reviewed.

In general, this is:
$$\frac{(E_i/E_{wm})_t - (E_i/E_{wm})_{t-1}}{(E_i/E_{wm})_{t-1}}$$

where E_i is employment of group i.

JOINT CENTER BOOKS OF RELATED INTEREST

For an up-to-date catalog of Joint Center books and reports, write:
  Book Orders, Joint Center for Political and Economic Studies,
  1090 Vermont Avenue, NW, Suite 1100, Washington, DC 20005.